Op... & shut

Also by
JOHN IBBITSON

NON-FICTION

The Polite Revolution: Perfecting the Canadian Dream

Loyal No More: Ontario's Struggle for a Separate Destiny

Promised Land: Inside the Mike Harris Revolution

YOUNG ADULT FICTION

The Landing

1812: Jeremy and the General

Open & Shut

Why America Has Barack Obama,
and Canada Has Stephen Harper

JOHN

IBBITSON

McClelland & Stewart

LIBRARY AND ARCHIVES CANADA CATALOGUING IN PUBLICATION

Ibbitson, John
Open and shut : why America has Barack Obama, and
Canada has Stephen Harper / John Ibbitson.

ISBN 978-0-7710-4318-5

1. Harper, Stephen, 1959-. 2. Obama, Barack. 3. Canada – Politics and government – 2006-. 4. United States – Politics and government – 2001-. 5. Prime ministers – Canada – Election. 6. Canada. Parliament – Elections, 2008. 7. Presidents – United States – Election – 2008. 8. United States. Congress – Elections, 2008. I. Title.

FC640.I23   2009 971.07'3   C2009-901234-0

We acknowledge the financial support of the Government of Canada through the Book Publishing Industry Development Program and that of the Government of Ontario through the Ontario Media Development Corporation's Ontario Book Initiative. We further acknowledge the support of the Canada Council for the Arts and the Ontario Arts Council for our publishing program.

Typeset in Perpetua by M&S, Toronto
Printed and bound in Canada

ANCIENT FOREST
FRIENDLY

This book is printed on acid-free paper that is 100% recycled, ancient-forest friendly (40% post-consumer recycled).

McClelland & Stewart Ltd.
75 Sherbourne Street
Toronto, Ontario
M5A 2P9
www.mcclelland.com

1 2 3 4 5   13 12 11 10 09

For Barry Bartmann,
wise guide

To make a government requires no great prudence. Settle the seat of power, teach obedience, and the work is done. To give freedom is still more easy. It is not necessary to guide; it only requires to let go the rein. But to form a free government, that is, to temper together these opposite elements of liberty and restraint in one consistent work, requires much thought, deep reflection, a sagacious, powerful, and combining mind.

EDMUND BURKE
Reflections on the
Revolution in France

Is there anything by which you can trace the marks of freedom, or discover those of wisdom? No wonder then Mr. Burke has . . . endeavored to lead his readers from the point by a wild, unsystematical display of paradoxical rhapsodies.

THOMAS PAINE
The Rights of Man

CONTENTS

Introduction

TOM PAINE WAS MAD.

The English writer and polemicist had considered Edmund Burke a supporter and friend. In his writings and from his seat in parliament, Burke had championed the Americans in their struggle for independence. Paine, while living in the United States, had written *Common Sense*, the bible of that revolution.

Now there was another revolution, in France, but this time Burke was vehemently opposed, arguing in *Reflections on the Revolution in France*, "A perfect democracy is the most shameless thing in the world," in which the masses exercise "an unnatural, inverted domination."

When *Reflections* was published in November 1791, Paine read it in a day and started writing his rebuttal the day after. He finished Part One of *The Rights of Man* the following February; the publisher had it out in March.

"What are the present Governments of Europe but a scene of iniquity and oppression?" Paine thundered. " . . . [A] general revolution in the principle and construction of Governments is necessary."

Burke versus Paine. We're still sorting it out.

The Rights of Man was a best-seller, and perhaps the greatest of an extinct literary genre, the political pamphlet. From the mid-seventeenth to the early nineteenth century, these quickly written and published polemics thrived wherever a reasonably free press was permitted, to be read and argued over in the ubiquitous coffee houses – at one point in the 1700s, London alone had more than five hundred – where everyone and their friends met to exchange gossip, get the news, and debate the folly of the powers-that-were.

By the mid-nineteenth century, pamphlets were in decline, eclipsed by newspapers, which were cheaper, more timely, and more reliable. Today, the political pamphlet is the last refuge of the to-the-ramparts! youth activist or the grim anti-abortionist on his determined corner.

Bloggers often argue that their postings are the new political pamphlet, and the Internet, the coffee houses of our time. But there is a profound difference between the daily – or hourly – musings of a political blog and a sustained argument of several thousands of words swiftly composed, and swiftly – by conventional standards – published, that seeks to draw lessons from the great events of the time.

Which is what I've set out to do with *Open & Shut.*

This book is an argument and an invitation. The argument is political. Canada and the United States each held federal elections in late 2008. The United States had been through eight years of calamity and mal-government. The administration of George W. Bush handled the worst terrorist attack in history, Hurricane Katrina, and a financial panic with even-handed incompetence. The forty-third president left his country in a shambles.

But America is the most resilient of nations. Just as it has produced disastrous presidents, so, too, it has responded to those disasters with great presidents. Right after taking office, President Barack Obama moved swiftly and emphatically to prevent a crippling recession from sinking into depression, while retooling the economic fundamentals of the federal government, seeking to curb America's contribution to global warming, launching landmark reforms in health care and education, and reversing the restrictions on stem-cell research. The opening days of his administration rivalled Roosevelt's.

Three weeks before the American election, Canadians went to the polls. The result of the fortieth Canadian general election was as flaccid as the campaign itself: a strengthened Conservative minority government, accompanied by the dispatch of what is turning into the annual leader of the Liberal Party of Canada.

But excitement was soon to come, as Prime Minister Stephen Harper, misreading both the economic and political times, ignored the financial slough the nation was falling into and instead tried to hobble the opposition parties' fundraising abilities. He almost lost the government as a result. Now he faces a new challenger, public intellectual Michael Ignatieff, who shares with Obama more than a name with many vowels. Once again, instability is the order of the day.

The elections and their aftermaths tell us two

things. For all its many faults, both structural and cultural, America's political fundamentals remain robust and renewable, allowing the nation to shake off the worst of its own excesses and put itself back on the right track. But in Canada, something has gone wrong. The always-fragile national will has atrophied, revealed in a political culture that, at the federal level, smells of decay.

Predicting the breakup of Canada is like predicting Armageddon. Every generation, febrile zealots take to the street corners, shrieking themselves hoarse with their prognostications of doom. But the appointed date for the end of the world, or the country, passes once again without incident, and the prophets shuffle home as a new batch takes their place on the soapboxes.

Canada, however, has had a few close calls with the apocalypse in recent decades: the 1970 FLQ crisis, the rise to power of René Lévesque in 1976, and the near-death referendum of November 1995. To stave off Confederation's oblivion, the federal government, under both the Conservatives and the Liberals, has steadily devolved many of its powers to the provinces. For the main, this has been a good thing: Ottawa is notoriously incompetent at managing social programs; the provinces needed the mandate and resources to do their job.

But things have gone too far. Ottawa is in the midst of a crisis of competence. The political class is a wraith of its former self. There is not a shadow of the statesman left in our politicians, nor much notion of public service in our public servants. The federal power is steadily weakening, losing legitimacy, surrendering a national vision to parochial interests.

After the inauguration, Michelle Obama visited various departments of the federal public service to thank the workers there for their efforts and to explain her husband's plans and priorities. At every gathering, the reception was rapturous. The wife of the president mingled with an enthused and rededicated public service. At the same time in Ottawa, a demonstrably incompetent government – or so the events of November and December 2008 suggest – huddled resentfully in the catacombs of the Langevin Block, while a moribund and hostile public service waited for someone to come along who could give it something to do. This is a really good way to wreck a country.

That may not be how you see the state of our nation. It may not be how you see it even after you have finished reading this little book. Maybe you have ideas of your own about where we are, how we got there, and where we should go next. That's where the invitation comes in.

The *Globe and Mail* has partnered with McClelland & Stewart to host an Internet forum for *Open & Shut* readers. At the end of this book, I'll explain how you can become part of a discussion based on the ideas and questions raised in the following pages. The goal is for you to advance the argument, or maybe to reshape it. I'll be reporting the results in an article for the *Globe*. Together, let's show the world that the art of the political pamphlet hasn't been lost after all.

We'll be looking together at what last fall's elections told us about the political cultures of Canada and the United States. We'll track the deterioration of both the political parties and the bureaucracy in this country. We'll examine the sorry state of the Canada–U.S. border. And we'll consider the shape of our cities and our schools, where the Americans also have something to teach us.

One of the most effective, if hypocritical, Canadian strategies is to criticize the United States with smug superiority and then steal its best ideas. It's time to repeat the exercise. Canada needs to strengthen its national government and renew its political culture by borrowing from some of the better angels of the American political nature. And we need to do it now, before it's too late.

Chapter 1

Two Elections

THE AMANA COLONIES form a collection of villages just south of Cedar Rapids, Iowa. All together, 1,600 souls live there. By the time of the 2008 Iowa caucuses on January 3, virtually every presidential candidate for both the Republicans and the Democrats had visited at least once. And they hadn't gone there to deliver a stump speech at a rally. They sat down at the local community centre or school gym, talking with whoever was interested in looking them over, making their pitch, then taking as many questions as people felt like asking. If you want to be the leader of the free world, first you have to convince Amana.

Many Canadians look with amused contempt on the American primary system. A bunch of farmers in an insignificant Midwestern state exercises enormous influence over who becomes president of the United States. Huge states such as New York and California have far less say in the outcome. The rules are hopelessly confusing and vary from state to state. And just what is a caucus, anyway?

In fact, the American system of choosing party leaders is far more open, inclusive, and democratic than the Canadian model. In the United States, a relative outsider such as Barack Obama – or Bill Clinton or Jimmy Carter – little known and, initially, with little money, can capture his party's nomination despite the entrenched opposition of the party establishment. That could never happen in Canada. There could never be a Prime Minister Barack Obama.

Until December 2007, almost all the pundits agreed that Hillary Clinton would win the nomination for the Democratic Party. The New York senator and former first lady led Obama by twenty points or more in the national polls and in most of the key early states. The other half-dozen candidates, from North Carolina senator John Edwards to Delaware senator Joe Biden, weren't even in the game.

And Hillary Clinton owned the Democratic Party. Her husband, Bill, remained its alpha male even after he left the presidency in 2001. Everyone, it was said, owed either Bill or Hillary or, most likely, both a favour. From a Georgia precinct captain to chair of the Democratic National Committee, they had their jobs because the Clintons chose them. The superdelegates – elected and senior party officials who made up 20 per cent of all the delegates to the Democratic National Convention – were in her corner. She was the inevitable candidate.

What the Clintons didn't understand, what almost no one understood, was that charisma married to new technology could render the inevitable impossible. Barack Obama was a political force of nature waiting to be unleashed. This child of a Kenyan father and a more-than-usually-liberal-for-Kansas-born mother, who was born in Hawaii (where his parents had met), who spent part of his childhood in Jakarta (after his mother left her first husband and married an Indonesian), and who was then shipped back to Hawaii (where his white grandparents raised him for a while), miraculously did not enter his twenties screaming with rage and agony over his identity. Instead, he matured into a stellar student, community organizer, first black president of the *Harvard Law Review*, and relentlessly ambitious politician who was chasing the presidency after only a year in the Senate.

He had an ability to galvanize supporters that had never before been witnessed. "I've seen only one similar national swoon," conservative columnist Charles Krauthammer told a no-doubt-mystified readership in the *Washington Post*. "As a teenager growing up in Canada, I witnessed a charismatic law professor go from obscurity to justice minister to prime minister, carried on a wave of what was called Trudeaumania."William Jennings Bryan's loyal legions of farmers, Adlai Stevenson's attraction to liberal intellectuals and women of a certain age, John F. Kennedy's urbane charm, even Ronald Reagan's folksy eloquence – they paled beside Obama's attributes. This guy had something that even now no one has successfully defined: a cool intelligence, a formal, almost old-fashioned prose style that, matched to his years watching black preachers move their congregations to hallelujahs and amens, gave him a command of oratory that could bring stadiums filled with tens of thousands to their feet and to tears.

And he had a personal appeal, the all-important quality of making whoever was talking to him feel that her words were being taken to heart. He performed badly during the all-candidates debates that dominated the summer and fall of 2007, looking uncertain and professorial. But in those Iowa town halls, the people who met him were impressed with this African-American professor and lawyer who, by all the laws of politics, should have left those Iowa farmers cold.

That is the genius of Iowa. The state is, in effect, a jury, where small gatherings of voters listen to the candidates, take the measure of the political testimony on offer, and then pronounce. Being in the middle of America, they are undistracted by the regional bickerings of Miami or New York or Los Angeles. Most of the time, no one pays any attention to them, but they listen acutely to what everyone everywhere is saying. Canadians know exactly how that feels.

The pundits didn't notice Obama's growing popularity in Iowa. They also didn't observe, at least not closely enough, his amazing fundraising ability. Even running a distant second to Hillary Clinton, he matched or exceeded her in raising money. But it wasn't just how much he was raising, it was how he was raising it.

Obama had tapped the latent energy of an entire generation of new voters, many of whom were profoundly disconnected from politics. Gen-Xers and Millennials were used to talking to one another through online social-networking and video websites that permitted a rich sharing of information and connections. Through Facebook, MySpace, Twitter, and YouTube, millions of young potential voters chatted, courted, and shared information and opinions. They didn't talk politics much, though they were vehemently opposed to the war in Iraq and to the Bush administration in general. And a growing number of them were voicing their enthusiasm for Barack Obama. He rode that enthusiasm to the White House.

David Axelrod, David Plouffe, Robert Gibbs, and Obama's other senior advisers knew that he could never become the Democratic presidential nominee by appealing to the party's establishment. It belonged to Hillary. What they could do was tap the social networks of the Internet to capture the nomination from outside the party. As the ranks of young supporters swelled, joined by affluent urban liberals enthused by this young, cool, cerebral yet inspiring black man's message of hope and renewal, Obama's campaign managers put them to work, creating a new, Internet-based grassroots movement that transformed American electoral politics.

When the first paid staffer arrived in Idaho to organize the state for its upcoming caucuses, he found a volunteer Idaho-for-Obama organization already in place. Its members had organized themselves online, through Facebook and MySpace. They had downloaded resources from the national campaign website, mapped out precincts, even chosen a campaign headquarters. The Obama machine encouraged these spontaneous movements, providing volunteers with voters lists and canvassing materials and advice. It's no coincidence that Obama's team recruited one of the creators of Facebook to run the online side of the campaign.

The volunteers encouraged one another and drew new recruits through unauthorized videos as sophisticated a will.i.am's *Yes We Can* and as cheesily effective as the Net sensation Obama Girl. And they raised money like nobody's business. Over the twenty-two months of Obama's primary and election campaigns, his supporters donated $750 million, a figure several times that raised by any candidate, ever. The average donation was less than a hundred dollars.

They shocked Clinton's organizers and supporters in January 2008 as they flooded into the community centres, school gyms, and living rooms of Iowa, muscling aside the Clinton contingent and handing Obama the state, transforming the election and setting the punditocracy back on its heels. If a state of white farmers and townsfolk could support an African-American candidate, then who else might vote for him?

Clinton rallied to take New Hampshire, the all-important first primary state. But now the larger population started to galvanize behind Obama. African Americans, who had mostly supported Hillary Clinton in the conviction that no black man could win the nomination or the election, listened to the message from Iowa and massively swung their vote behind Obama. While women largely held their allegiance to the New York senator, an increasing number of men of all races decided the man from Illinois would get their vote.

The proportional-representation system, by which states award delegates to the national convention according to the percentage of the vote each candidate receives, kept Obama competitive on Super Tuesday, when more than twenty states held primaries and caucuses simultaneously. And then the organizing power of the Obama campaign kicked in, resulting in eleven consecutive caucus and primary victories, unanswered by an exhausted and disoriented Clinton campaign.

She did eventually rally and fight back, but the outcome was no longer in doubt. Facing the inevitable, the superdelegates began trickling, then flooding to Obama's side. After everyone else – the young, the urban, liberals, labour — had joined with Obama's cause, the elite of the Democratic Party, conceding defeat, decided to nominate a black man and hope for the best.

The best was yet to come.

It takes two years, from the day after the mid-term elections until the day of the general election, to choose a president. In Canada, the run-up to the 2008 election seemed just as endless.

Stephen Harper's minority Conservative government victory in January 2006 promptly launched the Liberal Party on a search for yet another leader. After endless debates and delegate-selection battles, the party convened in Montreal at the end of November with four candidates given more-or-less equal odds. But Gerard Kennedy botched his floor management, Bob Rae was too new minted a Liberal, ditto Michael Ignatieff, who'd been out of the country most of his adult life, and so Stéphane Dion walked away with the prize, prompting the swiftest bout of buyers' remorse in political history when people realized that the austere academic was humourless, managerially incompetent, and barely intelligible in English.

Month after month, the nation teetered. The Conservatives edged toward majority-government territory in the polls, only to drop back to previous levels. The Opposition threatened to bring down the government on this or that, only to retreat when its bluff was called. Finally, last September, Harper decided it was October 14 or never, and visited the Governor General.

Suddenly, Canadian politics looked old. In provincial capitals and especially at the federal level, the leadership seemed weak, white, and bland. During the primary campaign, the vibrancy of American democracy was reflected in the Republican Party by candidates as varied as evangelist Mike Huckabee and former New York mayor Rudy Giuliani. The Democrats had to choose between the first woman presidential nominee and the first African-American presidential nominee. What were Canadians being offered? An overweight economist who couldn't offer an honest smile to save his life and a backpacking political scientist whose English made your ears bleed.

It wasn't as though Canada was having an off year. Politics at the federal level had been nothing but intra-party warfare punctuated by dispiriting elections for more than a decade. By the late 1990s, Paul Martin's quest to get Jean Chrétien to step down had taken on the qualities of a guerrilla campaign: shadowy, unpredictable, and vicious. The Conservative Party had split into three, and two of the three splinters also fell to warring, as Preston Manning tried to morph the Reform Party into the Canadian Alliance only to lose his leadership of the party to Stockwell Day, who lost it in turn to Stephen Harper. The Progressive Conservatives devoted much of their waning energies to ousting leader Joe Clark. Peter MacKay finally took the dubious prize, then discovered that it wasn't worth anything. He succumbed to Harper's offer of reunion, and to his leadership as well.

Meanwhile, Paul Martin, having finally reached the top of the greasy Liberal pole, betrayed a chronic indecisiveness that, coupled with a particularly nasty pay-to-play scandal in Quebec, soured voters on both him and his party. By 2006, Harper was prime minister, and the lead-up to the dispiriting 2008 election was underway.

Ottawa has seldom dazzled, but never had it looked so grey. Meanwhile, south of the border, Americans were mesmerized by the election of a lifetime.

In retrospect, John McCain never had a chance. After all, Hillary Clinton was competing with Obama to see which candidate would confront the Republican nominee. McCain was that nominee, which meant he inherited the toxic legacy of his predecessor, George W. Bush.

The United States is in crisis – the worst, many believe, since the Great Depression and the Second World War. Some of us, who remember Vietnam, the assassinations, Watergate, stagflation, the race riots, the oil shocks, and the hostage crisis in Iran, are not so sure. But there is no doubt that something is terribly, fundamentally wrong.

The attacks of September 11 unhinged many Americans. They certainly unhinged its president. George W. Bush threw his country into an invasion of Iraq in search of weapons of mass destruction that didn't exist and then let that unhappy country descend into civil war. The administration perverted the constitution: torturing, wiretapping, incarcerating, and deporting terrorist suspects to the tender mercies of barbarous regimes. To give it all a veneer of legality, the Bushites perverted the Justice Department, employing patronage and perverse legal reasoning to procure opinions that justified their actions. We even learned in March 2009 that government lawyers had advised the president after September 11 that he could suspend First Amendment rights to free speech on the grounds that the United States was in a state of war. The republic was in danger of turning into everything it had been founded in opposition to.

Meanwhile, twenty-five years of relentless deregulation had reached a tipping point. Unscrupulous agents were feeding unpayable mortgages to greedy home buyers who would never have qualified in any sane market, and these mortgages had dispersed through the global financial system, further worsening the balance sheets of companies and countries that were already running on nothing but credit. The bubble burst in 2007, and the real economy slumped into recession in 2008. America was going down, and it was taking the rest of the world with it.

All John McCain had to do was convince Americans that they should vote Republican again anyway.

Like Obama, McCain exploited the idiosyncrasies of the primary system to construct a campaign that snatched the nomination from the perceived front-runners. Actually, it's a bit more complicated than that. McCain had a long and well-deserved reputation as a maverick within his own party: a fiscal conservative, he nonetheless sponsored legislation to provide a path to citizenship for illegal immigrants; championed campaign finance reform; believed global warming was real; and opposed torture as a state policy, having experienced it first-hand in Vietnam.

But McCain had changed. In 2000, he was the outsider challenging establishment candidate George W. Bush. In 2007, he *was* the establishment, the man to beat in a crowded Republican field. Then, in the summer of 2007, his campaign imploded, brought down by overspending, underfundraising, and bad management. McCain retreated to New Hampshire, forgotten, while the establishment warred over who should replace him: Mitt Romney? (A Mormon, and rather strange.) Rudy Giuliani? (Liberal on abortion, and former mayor of Babylon.) Mike Huckabee? (Too religious, if such a thing is possible in the GOP, and too populist to boot.)

While they agonized, forgotten John worked New Hampshire, trying to shake hands with every potential Republican voter in the state, bumming rides, holding an endless series of town hall meetings.

Come January 8, 2008, New Hampshire cast its vote for McCain, and suddenly the maverick was a front-runner again. New Hampshire gave him

South Carolina, and South Carolina gave him Florida, and Florida gave him Super Tuesday, and then it was all over, though Mike Huckabee hung in for a while, just to improve his name recognition and speaker's fees.

But now McCain faced the near-impossible challenge of overcoming the legacy of Iraq, Katrina, Abu Ghraib, Guantanamo, Wall Street – everything that had made George W. Bush one of the least popular presidents in history, a man ranked with Herbert Hoover, James Buchanan, and Rutherford B. Hayes in the pantheon of failure – of rebranding himself and his party, and defeating a charismatic and deeply intelligent Democratic nominee in command of a fundraising and organizational machine unlike any witnessed anywhere in history. McCain had only one hope: that blue-collar workers in the industrial states of the upper Midwest wouldn't vote for a black man. It seemed a reasonable hope at the time. The idea that a country that was less than two generations past Jim Crow, whose cities are still scarred with black ghettoes, where mutual resentment and suspicion still define the black-white relationship was ready to elect a black man seemed hard to believe. Hell, a year earlier it had seemed inconceivable.

McCain did everything he could with the race card, short of playing it. He derided Obama as The One: an exotic celebrity whose values were alien to average (read: white, working-class) Americans. He played up Obama's slender ties to William Ayers, a university professor who, back in the day, had led the Weather Underground, a largely inept war-resistance movement that had accidentally killed a policeman. And he chose Sarah Palin, good-old governor of Alaska, as his running mate. Palin was hugely popular with the Republican base, as she gosh-darned her way around the country, cheerfully extolling the small-town values "of what I call the real America."

Who knows if it might have worked? At one point, in September, the two campaigns were tied in the polls. But then the markets went south, Lehman Brothers went belly up, John McCain suspended his campaign and went to Washington for no good reason, and the voters went to Obama.

McCain was swamped by events and by the Obama machine, which focused obsessively on registering new voters and then getting them to vote. Sixty-one per cent of eligible voters cast a ballot on November 4, the highest turnout since the epic election of 1968. Ten per cent of those voters hadn't cast a ballot in 2004, because they had been too young, they had not registered to vote, or were registered but had stayed home anyway. These new arrivals to the polling booths voted two-to-one for Barack Obama over John McCain. They, along with the almost unanimous support of black voters and the two-thirds support of Latinos, were crucial to Obama's victory.

And those blue-collar voters in Pennsylvania and Michigan and Ohio and Indiana, well, they did something remarkable. They didn't overcome their racial resentments, they just set them aside. They could see that Obama was smart and together and ready to lead, and that McCain was old, desperate, and prone to making rash, bad decisions. In the middle of an economic crisis, the choice was clear.

It's easy for an upper-income, university-educated liberal living in a major city to vote for a black candidate. But for a white mill worker in Cleveland to cast such a vote – that was heroic.

On election night, hundreds of thousands of ecstatic supporters cheered wildly as the networks declared Obama elected. Across the nation and around the world, there were tears of joy. America had once again proven its critics wrong. Sure, the economic crisis was still there; sure, there were still troops in Iraq and prisoners in Guantanamo, but all that was about to change. At least, people believed it was about to change. As one observer put it: Americans' relentless optimism keeps getting them into trouble, and that same relentless optimism keeps getting them out of it.

"If there is anyone out there who still doubts that America is a place where all things are possible," Obama declared that night, "who still wonders if the dream of our founders is alive in our time; who still questions the power of our democracy, tonight is your answer." Yes it was.

Canadians knew who they were voting for as well: Stephen Harper had been in and out of federal politics since 1993 and prime minister for nearly three years. Stéphane Dion they knew through his years in Chrétien's government spent battling Quebec separatists. NDP leader Jack Layton was embarking on his third federal election. The Bloc Québécois's Gilles Duceppe was fighting his fifth.

All of these men had been picked by a tiny elite: card-carrying party members, a fraction of 1 per cent of the electorate for each party. In the case of the Conservatives, Stephen Harper himself had negotiated the conditions that led to the creation of the party he dominated. In the case of the Liberals, Stéphane Dion's operatives had simply outmanoeuvred his rivals on the convention floor.

As the election progressed, apathy turned to resignation. Dion's carbon tax, if that's what it was, was incomprehensible. Stephen Harper ridiculed the Liberal climate initiative but had even less to offer in response. For a while, it looked as though the Conservatives might pull off a majority. Dion actually managed to perform below expectations, low though they were. Elizabeth May's Green Party was doing well, threatening to further split the left. Hopeful Tory loyalists began to whisper to one another: *four more years?*

But Harper has the peculiar genius of being able to plan strategically brilliant campaigns and then to self-immolate. As the global financial system threatened to implode, he told voters to look at their melting portfolios as "a buying opportunity." When critics called him a philistine for some innocuous cuts to arts funding, he responded that "ordinary working people" get pissed off when they watch artists on television attending some "rich gala all subsidized by taxpayers claiming their subsidies aren't high enough." Quebecers take the arts seriously. The Bloc Québécois rebounded.

After five dispiriting weeks: a new Parliament same as the old Parliament, with voter turnout down to 59 per cent, the worst ever. The Tories gained some seats but not enough to form a majority government. The Liberals lost enough seats to doom Stéphane Dion but held on as official opposition. The Greens went nowhere, and the Bloc remained strong in Quebec. Stalemate.

Things should have gone on like that for a couple of years before election fever – well, fever is a strong word to describe the political temperature in Ottawa these days – returned. Instead, Stephen Harper managed to foment a constitutional crisis when his finance minister's economic statement pretty much ignored the threatening global depression and focused instead on stripping parties of public funding, which would have destroyed the Liberals, NDP, and Bloc.

The Liberals and the NDP agreed to form a coalition, which the Bloc agreed to support. They would bring down the Tories and install Stéphane Dion as leader, even though he had already announced his

resignation and a Liberal leadership race was underway. Canadians were appalled. Stephen Harper may
not be loveable, but he is at least generally regarded
as smart. But he was now on the brink of losing power
over his obsessive need to damage his political oppo-
nents by foul means or fouler. He'd acted like an idiot.
Nonetheless, nobody, but nobody, had voted for a
Liberal-NDP coalition. Yet now it seemed this was the
government they were going to get. Scholars calmly
explained that this is how parliamentary democracy
works. Nuts, said the voters. Ultimately, Harper
rescued his government by convincing Governor
General Michaëlle Jean to prorogue Parliament until
the end of January. (There were constitutional prece-
dents for her to have ignored his advice and demand
he meet the House. But the Governor General reads
the newspapers.) That gave the Liberals time to
replace Dion with Michael Ignatieff and for saner
heads to ensure that the Tory budget, when it arrived
January 26, would survive a vote of confidence. The
government staggered on.

Intolerance isn't why Barack Obama could never
become prime minister of Canada. There is no reason

to believe Canadians are any more racist than their American cousins. (Though there is also no good reason to believe they are less so.) Barack Obama could not become prime minister because the American political system is open, while in Canada, it's shut. American political culture is marked by curiosity, experiment, and lively – sometimes fierce – debate. Politics in Canada is cautious and consensual. The American republic is as young as the Declaration of Independence; Canada's parliamentary democracy is as old as the Magna Carta. The role of the people in electing governments promotes change and diversity in the United States, while in Canada, political elites ensure that most of the time Canadians get mostly the same.

Barack Obama is the first African-American president of the United States. (Properly speaking, he's biracial and not a descendent of slaves, which is central to the African-American experience. But that truth is outside this argument.) Had Obama lost the Democratic nomination, America would probably be celebrating the election of the first woman president, Hillary Clinton.

Currently, eight of the fifty states are governed by women. (The record, reached twice, is nine.) Arizona has had three women governors in a row, and from different parties. Two state governors are black (one of them, New York's appointed governor, David Peterson, is also blind) and Bill Richardson of New Mexico is Latino. And in 2007, Bobby Jindal (his real first name is Piyush) became the first Indo-American governor – of Louisiana, no less. Some observers believe Jindal could become the Republican presidential nominee in 2012 – and wouldn't that leave the good ole boys in a pickle – though the abysmal delivery of his response to Obama's magisterial first address to Congress on February 24 didn't help his chances.

Stephen Harper is the first nothing-at-all. All of Canada's first ministers are white men. Catherine Callbeck of Prince Edward Island is the only woman ever elected premier, and its current premier, Robert Ghiz, is of (distant) Lebanese extraction, but apart from that island – not otherwise noted for its diversity – Canadian politics remains lily white. (Leaders from territories and dependencies have been excluded in both cases.)

The nature of the American political system makes it possible for outsiders to challenge party elites. In Canada, political elites are protected by the parliamentary system and by Canada's closed political culture. Those elites almost entirely consist of white men, and while they insist it isn't true, they favour their own kind.

Some Canadian political parties have mandates aimed at increasing the number of female candidates, but that simply proves the point: diversity in Canadian politics, to the extent it exists, is imposed from the top down. But Nancy Pelosi became Speaker of the House of Representatives and one of the most powerful politicians in the United States all by herself.

Let's go back to Iowa. In those all-important first caucuses, only about 6 per cent of eligible voters typically show up, although three times that number took part in the 2008 caucuses. Turnout at caucuses is usually low because it's an all-evening affair, in which voters publically declare their support for their favoured candidate, and there can be several votes over the course of the evening.

Because the Iowa jury consists of a small number of politically engaged voters who spend a lot of time listening and talking to the candidates before making up their minds, Hillary Clinton's high visibility and months of organizing couldn't help her. And the aura of inevitability that her campaign cultivated didn't go down well in a state that enjoys upsetting the inevitable. She placed third.

Hearing from the politically engaged base of your party is what caucuses are about. Hearing from the broader population is what primaries are about. Clinton rebounded from losing Iowa to win New Hampshire. New Hampshire is an open primary, which means that anyone – registered Democrats, Republicans, and independents – can vote in the primary of their choice. Voters in the Granite State are a contrary lot, and they were unimpressed with the messianic coverage that Obama had enjoyed since his Iowa win. Sixty-three per cent of voters turned out, reviving Clinton's campaign and galvanizing John McCain's.

Mitt Romney, who spent a large portion of his considerable fortune in these states, lost both. You can't buy Iowa and New Hampshire. You have to earn them.

Winning either of these small states can give an outsider a credible shot at his or her party's nomination. Winning New Hampshire in 2000 made John McCain a serious contender for the Republican nomination. Coming second in New Hampshire in 1992 made Bill Clinton the Comeback Kid. Sure, money helps; sure, party connections help. But in American politics, money, and connections need not be decisive. Because everyone has a right to vote for the party's nominee, politicians can go over the head of the party bosses and appeal directly to the electors. If those electors like what they see, the candidate is on his or her way; if they don't, goodbye John Edwards and Rudy Giuliani.

In Canada, only 1 to 2 per cent of Canadians belong to a political party at any one time, gaming the system in favour of party elites. Party members tend to be better educated, older, and male. So during any Liberal or Conservative leadership contest, only a minuscule and unrepresentative portion of the Canadian electorate gets to participate.

Why is that? Why don't more Canadians belong to political parties? For one thing, we don't make them. Voters in the United States must register as Democrat, Republican, or independent. (The numbers of independents has swelled in recent decades from 2 per cent of registered voters in the early 1960s to 22 per cent in 2004.) Joining a Canadian political party usually costs ten dollars, and there's no reason to join unless you want to participate in choosing a leader, and to do that, you may have to participate in the Canadian equivalent of caucuses.

The Liberals choose their leaders by holding delegate selection meetings in all 308 ridings. Delegates are apportioned based on the number of votes cast at the meeting for each candidate. So if you want some say in choosing the Liberal leader, that means hours of commitment on your part. You may even have to endure speeches.

The Conservatives choose their delegates slightly differently. Members simply cast ballots in their ridings, with points awarded based on the percentage of votes cast, rather like the way the Democrats choose delegates based on state votes. But the Conservative method is, in fact, wildly undemocratic. In Democratic primaries, California is entitled to 379 delegates and Wyoming to twelve, because California is home to a great many more people than Wyoming. But in the Conservative contest, every riding sends the same number of delegates. That would be fair if the voter base were the general population, but Conservative Party members are not equally distributed. When the reunified Conservative Party held its first convention in 2004, Quebec was allotted 25 per cent of the available points, even though only 9,000 of the party's 252,000 members lived in Quebec. Belinda Stronach tried to seize the leadership of the party by recruiting

new members in Quebec – a strategy that failed only
because no one inside Quebec (or outside) thought she
was fit to lead the party.

Leaders from the outside have taken over political parties: Lester Pearson, Pierre Trudeau, Brian
Mulroney. But they all commanded sizeable constituencies within the party. The fact remains that it
is virtually impossible for someone not approved by
a political party's internal leadership structure –
from the federal caucus and the national executive
all the way down to the heads of the local riding associations – to seize the leadership of that party. Take
the case of Valerie Chu.

By her early thirties, Chu had already made
her first 10 million as cofounder of a Vancouver-
based high-tech company. Bored with business and
worried about the state of the Canadian economy,
she sought and won the Liberal nomination for
British Columbia's legislative assembly in a downtown Vancouver riding, which she also easily took in
the next provincial election.

Impressed with her obvious intelligence and
engaging personality, the Liberal premier soon
promoted her to a minor portfolio in cabinet. But
Chu really came to the attention of Canadians when

36

she chose to attend the national Conservative leadership convention, where her ringing defence of multiculturalism and fiscal responsibility was the highlight of the event. When the Conservatives lost the next general election, Chu decided to run for the party leadership.

The odds were impossibly long. Worried by this rookie outsider, party officials decided to set a ninety-day cut-off for party memberships. Chu had put together a vibrant Netroots campaign driven by young and enthusiastic supporters that stretched across much of the country, and her fundraising was truly impressive. Opinion polls showed most Canadians thought she would be the best choice for the Conservatives. But her principal opponent had the support of most of the caucus and control of most of the riding associations, which meant he was the choice of the party faithful. There was simply no way that Chu could sell enough memberships to overwhelm the existing membership base in all 308 ridings. The fact that she was from British Columbia didn't help her in Quebec, even though her French was proficient. For Conservatives in Atlantic Canada, this charismatic Chinese Canadian from the West Coast might as well have been from a different country entirely.

Chu did well on the lower mainland and in Greater Toronto. Elsewhere, she was heavily outpolled. The Conservatives ultimately chose a slightly overweight middle-aged white man as leader.

Of course, there is no Valerie Chu, at least not one who's a rising star in Canadian politics. But if there were, this would be the probable outcome of her attempt to vault to the leadership of a political party. It is one reason (voting apathy among immigrants and the young is another) why Ontario and British Columbia have middle-aged white guys as premiers who lead cabinets that are overwhelmingly white as well, even though Toronto and Vancouver are rapidly turning into minority-majority cities (where ethnic minorities make up the majority of the population).

Parliamentary systems are geared to produce these results. In Great Britain, Australia, and New Zealand, party leaders are chosen by their caucus mates. As in so many other areas, Canada straddles the elite-driven society of Great Britain (and the rest of Europe) and the populism of the United States. But for better or worse, America is the country that, overwhelmingly, influences ours. We owe our Charter of Rights and Freedoms to Pierre Trudeau's determination to imitate the Bill of Rights in the American constitution. Fixed election dates are increasingly the law of the land. But anything that would make Canada more directly democratic meets tremendous resistance.

Take referendums. Americans love them. Every election, state ballots are larded with propositions that voters can approve or veto, and the result becomes law. They can be a nuisance or worse, especially since voters tend to support propositions that lower taxes and expand services. But they remain popular, and it would never occur to any legislature or political party to scrap them.

Canadian governments don't like referendums, simply because the results are rarely what the political elites desire. The Charlottetown Accord of 1992 was the last national one. Every party leader in the House of Commons and every premier endorsed that constitutional accord, which the people soundly voted down. This didn't convince those leaders to change their thinking. It simply increased their resolve to avoid referendums. In this we mirror Europeans, who avoid referendums as much as possible because the result is almost invariably disappointing for those in charge.

Political cultures reflect the larger cultures of which they are a vital part. Parliamentary government isn't inherently inferior or superior to Congressional government. The Australians have adapted their Westminster model to reflect their rambunctious society by employing a form of proportional representation. If Australia and America's political cultures are healthier than Canada's – and they are – then other forces must be at work bolstering theirs and weakening ours. So now let's talk about that.

Chapter 2

Open America; Closed Canada

AMERICAN SOCIETY IS OPEN; Canadian society is closed. Everyone who's lived in both countries knows this. It's impossible to quantify. It's just there. You don't sit alone for long in an American bar before someone asks you how you're doing. In a Canadian bar, you drink by yourself. In American government offices, the onus is on staff to provide information unless there's a reason not to; in Canada, the attitude is, "What business is it of yours?"

Earlier this year, North America was gripped by fears of tainted peanuts. Eight people died from salmonella that had contaminated products of the Peanut Corporation of America. Authorities on both sides of the border were first alerted to a possible problem when a Canadian company rejected a shipment of chopped peanuts from the company because they were putrid. An official at the U.S. Food and Drug Administration told my colleague Paul Koring that the Canadian Food Inspection Agency had tipped the Americans off about the problem peanuts. But when we contacted them, the CFIA refused to confirm the information. We shook our heads. Even for a story that would make Canadian officials look good, the government was unwilling to confirm information that Americans provided readily.

In late February, Paul revealed another case in point. The State Department had just issued its annual compendium of human rights around the world. This year's version pointed to torture, rape, and other horrific abuses inside Afghan prisons. As Koring noted in the *Globe and Mail*, "A similar annual Canadian report prepared by Foreign Affairs is heavily censored to remove all references to torture and abuse of detainees and the worst abuses in prisons. Each year, the U.S. report is public and posted on the Internet unexpurgated. The Canadian ones are only available under the Access to Information Act, and then only heavily redacted."

It's like that all the time.

———

Clichés are clichés because they're true. America is a country forged in rebellion, and the animating spirit of that rebellion continues to shape its society and politics. Egalitarianism in the United States doesn't mean equal opportunity for all, much less that everyone gets an equal share. It means "Don't think you're better than me, because you're not, and I might have to punch you."

Canada evolved so slowly and respectfully from colony to country that it's impossible even to say for sure when we actually became sovereign. The Tory tradition of deference to one's betters, and the French tradition of deference to the Church, began to disappear only in the social revolutions of the 1960s. That decline of deference has gone pretty far, yet a reluctance toward openness remains part of Canadian life and political culture.

In exchange for a more closed society, Canadians traditionally have enjoyed a stability of government that Americans would, at certain periods of their history, have envied. Canada made it through the Great Depression, fought and helped win the Second World War, and forged a postwar society under the benevolent guidance of successive Liberal governments. Apart from the brief panic of the FLQ crisis,

Canada weathered the social and political upheavals of the 1960s and 1970s with no more social strife than the occasional sit-in at a university president's office. In the 1980s, no Reagans or Thatchers tore apart our social safety net.

But we are paying a price for that stability. Other settler societies rooted in the British political culture have found ways to open up their politics. The Australians have long embraced a class-based populism, making Aussies the most exuberant Anglo-Saxons on earth. New Zealand has served as a sort of political laboratory, leading the way in creating the welfare state, then in dismantling it, then in searching for something in between. But Canadians have resisted reform. It took until 1982 to bring home our Constitution, and repeated attempts to fix the Senate or clarify federal-provincial powers have come a cropper. Meanwhile, subterranean stresses – some very old, some quite recent – have been subtly undermining stability. In the past decade, the chickens have come home to roost, the bills have come due, the clichés are proving their worth. Politics at the federal level is in disarray, the political parties and their leaders are a shadow of their predecessors. And the country is paying a price.

———

Let's look, first, at the old stuff. Comparative historians tend to focus on founding documents, and it's true that the American and Canadian constitutions reflect the differing political cultures that produced them. The Declaration of Independence, the Constitution of 1787, and the Bill of Rights stress the sovereignty of the people, the rights of the individual, the determination not to vest power in one leader or even one arm of government. The British North America Act that governed Canada emphasized "peace, order and good government" and set up strong executives in both the federal and provincial parliaments. Over the years, and with the patriation of the Constitution, Canadian society has evolved away from the British model and toward the American. But ours remains a society that values order as much as freedom, where arguments in favour of the common good are likely to trump those defending individual liberty. They have low taxes and private health care; we have higher taxes and public health care. They bear arms; we have human rights commissions. You know all this.

Another great historical fact determined the differing shapes of American and Canadian political cultures: they had a civil war. We didn't. Maybe we should have, because politically the Civil War was the best thing that ever happened to the United States.

Both of our countries are federations: a collection of provinces or states yoked together by a central government. All federations everywhere grapple with the inherent ambiguities of split jurisdictions. Where do one government's responsibilities end and another's begin? What is the role for each level of government in areas of shared responsibility? From its founding until 1860, America struggled with another, far more vital, concern: should slavery be permitted to expand into the western territories and states? The dispute ultimately led to a civil war so bloody that more soldiers died in it than have died in all American wars since. Victory by the North in 1865 ensured that, from that time forward, the definition of the United States was the northern definition; the culture of the United States was primarily the northern culture. The American myth — we are an industrious, expansive, egalitarian and robustly free people — is a northern construct. Ironically, the decisive outcome of the war turned out to be a powerful unifier. To paraphrase historian Shelby Foote, people before the Civil War referred to the United States in the plural; after the Civil War they referred to it in the singular.

The Civil War settled another argument. At its end, the federal government was unquestionably The Government That Mattered. States' rights remain an issue in American politics, and states even have some powers that provinces lack – imagine Alberta deciding whether to restore the death penalty. But the states are clearly subordinate to the federal power. Many Canadian political theorists argue that Confederation was and is a contract among provinces, which agreed to create a weak federal government that would act on their behalf in matters of joint interest, but with the provinces sovereign in the spheres of their jurisdiction. This is called the Compact Theory of Confederation. There are no Compact Republic Americans.

Canada could have had a civil war. Anger over the crushing of the Riel Rebellion or over conscription during the First World War, or even the Second, could have pushed Quebec to attempt secession. We can only speculate on whether English Canada would have permitted it, or whether both sides would have raised armies and fought it out. We can only speculate as well about whether, assuming it was defeated, Quebec would have followed the South's example and sullenly accepted the English definition of the Canadian myth. Instead, our political leaders reached one compromise after another.

Along the way, several ideas became entrenched, prime among them that the provinces are the senior government when it comes to social policy; that any province can, if it so chooses, leave the federation peacefully, provided certain conditions are met; and that the federal power cannot and should not impose its will on the provinces in areas of domestic policy, but must instead seek their consent.

This, perhaps more than anything else, is why Canada is not, and never will become, a nation.

There are tremendous advantages to this absence of national cohesion. I began a previous book, *The Polite Revolution*, with this sentence: "Sometime, not too long ago, while no one was watching, Canada became the world's most successful country." I still believe this. Canada has evolved into a marvellous multi-ethnic, polyglot, urban, young, cosmopolitan society precisely because it has failed as a nation state. Our lack of a defining myth or single identity is what makes it possible for people from all over the world to come here and to live together in and around our major cities without any of them feeling as though they are The

Other. It is the fuel that set off the explosion of artistic and entrepreneurial talent that is reshaping twenty-first-century Canada. We may not cut it as a nation, but this is a great postnational country.

But there are forces at work that are eating away at the federal level of our politics and dysfunctions that are threatening to reach dangerous levels. Three elections in five years have produced three minority governments. Canadians seem to like minority governments, but Lord knows why. Stuff isn't getting done. And there is something badly, deeply wrong with both of our major political parties.

The Liberal Party is unrecognizable as the natural governing party that the older among us still remember. The rot, as some have observed, actually began to set in as far back as 1957, when John Diefenbaker eked out a minority government in part by virtually shutting the Liberals out of the West. The party became a stranger to everyone west of Ontario; it remains a stranger to this day. In 1984, the same thing happened in the former Liberal bastion of Quebec. In the francophone ridings outside Montreal and (what is now) Gatineau, Brian Mulroney's Progressive Conservatives swept the province. The Liberals have never recovered. Rather than uniting behind an effort to bridge Canada's deepening regional political divides, the Liberals engaged in more than twenty years of internal bickering and insurgency, demonstrating the very worst aspects of an elite-driven party estranged from and indifferent toward the electorate.

The Liberals' great strength in the 1990s was its hold on Ontario and Montreal. During the years of schism on the right, it enabled Chrétien to compile successive minority governments. But in 2004, a reunited Conservative Party began eroding the Liberals' base of support in Ontario. Today, the Liberal Party of Canada commands the political loyalties of voters in the country's three biggest cities – Toronto, Montreal, and Vancouver – with a smattering of ridings in Atlantic Canada. The real danger for the Liberals is that they accept this sorry state of affairs. Even as Howard Dean, chair of the U.S. Democratic National Committee, was convincing his party to pursue a fifty-state strategy – it forced the opposition to dissipate resources and exploited demographic shifts that played to the Democrats' advantage – the Liberal Party hunkered down in its disparate bastions, shuttered to the nation it seeks to govern. Today, the party is penniless, without direction, and on its fourth leader in five years. In the next election, if things go well, it may pick up enough seats in southwestern Ontario to eke out a minority government; if things go badly . . . It's painful to think of what could happen to the party then.

At least the Liberals have never tried to hide — well, not very hard — the elitism of their party's power structure. The Conservative Party of Canada, on the other hand, just lies about it.

The Progressive Conservatives always were an illogical party, exploiting Western, nationalist Québécois, and rural Ontario resentments, which is why they so rarely came to power. After the debacles of the Meech Lake and Charlottetown accords fractured the party in 1993, it took a decade before the English-speaking shards glued themselves together in a new Conservative Party, under Stephen Harper's leadership. The sponsorship scandal in Quebec, the growing internal disarray of the Liberal Party, and the public's general exhaustion with Liberal rule brought Harper to power in 2006 with a minority government, and a minority government it remained in 2008. The truth is, the Conservative Party is at least as weak and at risk of further decline as the Liberal Party, simply because it cannot resolve the fundamental paradox of its existence, which is embodied in the paradox that is Stephen Harper.

There are two parts to the Conservative Party. The smaller part is the Red Tory remnant. Red Tories believe everything that Liberals believe about social progress but from a sense of noblesse oblige. Some of them also retain a touching fondness for what used to be the British Empire. But apart from a few Celtic true believers in rural Atlantic Canada, Red Toryism is dead because its adherents are, or soon will be.

The larger chunk of the Conservative Party consists of Western rural populists, who created the Reform Party when the Progressive Conservatives imploded. Evangelical or fundamentalist in its religion – and this group actually has some – fiscally and socially conservative and strongly pro-American, the reform movement was also once strong in rural Upper Canada, and the Conservatives started their march back to power in 2004 by marrying their Western base to the remnant of reformers in southwestern Ontario. Reform should be a movement in decline, since its strongest adherents are found in rural ridings, and there is no future in rural votes in this ever-more-urban country. But Reform did find purchase in Calgary and Edmonton, which, until last fall, were the richest and fastest-growing places in the country. ("Please, Lord," they used to pray in Alberta, "just give me one more boom and I promise not to piss this one away." He listened. They pissed it away.)

Exploiting rural populism and resentments, even with Calgary and Edmonton onside, does not lead to majority government, not federally. National power lies in courting the social and fiscal moderates who live in the vast suburban belts around Toronto and Vancouver, along with as many Quebec nationalists as can be wooed from the embrace of the Bloc Québécois. The political balancing act for Stephen Harper has been to keep the Reform base of the party enthused – it is this base that contributes so handsomely to the party, giving the Conservatives an impressive financial edge at election time – while moderating his politics enough to appeal to suburban voters who may look askance at the Republican wannabes within the Tory ranks, but who are equally suspicious of the smug, pro-tax, metrosexual Liberals downtown.

Much of the time, Harper has been pretty skillful at reconciling, or maybe hoodwinking, both constituencies. But the paradox invariably reveals itself during elections, when statements and actions meant to placate the base — making fun of chardonnay-swilling *artistes* griping about cuts to their grants at taxpayer-funded galas — alarm the less philistine elements of the electorate. Five per cent of the population grudgingly slouches back to the Liberals — or, in Quebec, indignantly rushes into the embrace of the Bloc — and hopes for a real victory, a majority government, evaporate.

And now even the party's base feels deceived. Confronted by the worsening economy and December 2008's near-death experience for his government, Harper and his finance minister, Jim Flaherty, brought down a budget so laden with stimulus dollars that the loudest howls of indignation came from Harper's own supporters. "There's a lot of feeling of betrayal. We don't need a second Liberal Party," Tasha Kheiriddin, a conservative political scientist and pundit, told the *Globe and Mail.* "This is survival without any sense of direction," fumed Tom Flanagan, a former adviser to Harper, who went on to predict that the budget would harm Tory fundraising. Monte Solberg, who had been in Harper's cabinet, asked, "The Conservatives have easily escaped to fight another day, but what are they fighting for?"

As the snow banks piled ever higher beside Ottawa's driveways, it became increasingly clear that Stephen Harper, son of Reform, former self-described social conservative, the personification of populist, Western, neo-Republican alienation, had become a liberal. Who knew?

Both the Liberals and the Conservatives, then, are dangerously weak, each in their own way. And there are alarming signs — the December constitutional crisis being only the latest — that they are growing even weaker, more closed, and more remote from the interests and will of the people.

What's happening here? Why is the quality of leadership so lacklustre that fewer and fewer Canadians are even bothering to vote? Why do we seem incapable of electing a majority government, and why are our minority governments so chronically weak? Several things could be at work. In truth, probably all of them are.

First, there are the federal-provincial tides. Historically, power has ebbed and flowed between the federal government and the provinces. From Confederation until the First World War, it tended to flow from Ottawa downward. In modern times – after the Second World War – there was initially a long, sustained transfer of fiscal and political power upward to the federal level. Chronic deficits and fears of Quebec separation reversed those flows again, starting in the 1980s and leading right up to today.

One consequence is that provinces – at least Ontario and Quebec, with British Columbia and Alberta rapidly catching up – have all the money and experience they need – or as much as they have any right to expect – to operate their health care and education systems, to run welfare and manage the municipalities. With Ottawa mostly out of the subsidized housing game, with the transportation system downloaded or privatized, with the cultural industries maturing – at least, as much as they're ever going to mature – with social assistance now a purely provincial affair, with the provinces left almost completely in charge of settling and integrating immigrants, with, in short, the provinces doing most of the heavy lifting, there's little left to keep Ottawa busy. And so a managing-the-store mentality sets in.

While Barack Obama's administration sought to exploit the current economic crisis to attempt huge reforms in health care, education, the environment, and energy, the Harper government first tried to pretend there was no crisis, then offered the least possible amount of stimulus to avoid defeat in the House. The Liberals voted for the January budget with the greatest of reluctance. It hasn't occurred to the leadership of either party that this might be an opportunity to actually *do* something. Something big. High-speed rail from Windsor to Quebec City and Calgary to Edmonton. Grants, not loans, to make university, college, or apprenticeships universally affordable. Rural broadband or satellite access for the Internet. A new – oh, never mind.

A second reason the political parties are broken is that, with each new government, fewer people have more power. Reporters invariably write stories that begin: "Never before has so much power been concentrated in the hands of the prime minister and a few key advisers." Every such story is true. Pierre Trudeau's administration was more centralized than Lester Pearson's, and Brian Mulroney's government was more centralized than Trudeau's. Jeffrey Simpson of the *Globe and Mail* wrote a book describing Jean Chrétien's regime as "a friendly dictatorship," and Paul Martin created within the Privy Council Office a miniature parallel bureaucracy.

In Stephen Harper's government, centralization has reached previously unimaginable levels. Simpson calls him "El Commandante." Cabinet ministers speaking off the record describe an administration run, in essence, by two men: Harper and Kevin Lynch, Clerk of the Privy Council. All policy goes through them and their coterie of advisers, and much policy comes from them. No report is released, no interview granted, no press release issued unless "the Centre" has signed off on it. Veteran bureaucrats report that never before in their entire careers have they seen a government in which so much decision making is so tightly grasped in the hands of so few.

Under the circumstances, why would anyone with a brain and a spine run for public office? Members of Parliament are nonentities; efforts by the Paul Martin government to increase the influence and independence of parliamentary committees lasted about an hour after Stephen Harper moved into 24 Sussex. Ministers have become MPs with a car and driver. Harper's repeated cabinet shuffles reflect the instability and ineffectiveness of his cabinet. Its strongest members — Jim Flaherty, Jim Prentice, Stockwell Day, Peter MacKay — are weaker than any of their counterparts in previous governments.

The lure of politics is power: the ability to influence the public agenda. But if the federal government is turning into a not-so-friendly dictatorship, then what profiteth it a man or woman to become a part of it? Why not stay on Bay Street? Or work on education policy in Winnipeg? What does Ottawa have to offer except a lot of snow and grief from the PMO?

There is a third reason for the growing dysfunction of national politics, a reason so uncomfortable we don't even like to acknowledge it. The Bloc Québécois is trying to destroy Canada, and it's doing a pretty good job. Nationalist francophone voters in Quebec seem quite content to send fifty or so MPs to Parliament who are dedicated to pursuing the single object of gaining more and more powers for Quebec. The Bloc will sometimes co-operate on national issues, especially if they cater to its leftist social agenda. But the fundamental purpose of the Bloc is to advance the independence of Quebec.

The consequences are pernicious. The block of Bloc MPs makes it virtually impossible for either the

Conservatives or the Liberals to form a majority government. Its existence and its advocacy reinforce a politics of identity, of language, of region, of grievance. None of these are good for the political health of a country. And as the Bloc compels governing parties to pass power and responsibility to Quebec City, power and responsibility pass inevitably to Queen's Park and Edmonton and Victoria as well. Not only does Quebec go more and more its own way; every region goes more and more its own way. Quebec demands a seat at UNESCO; Alberta opens a trade office in Washington. Quebec demands even more from the equalization pot; Newfoundland declares political warfare over the Atlantic Accord. Ottawa is not only getting out of things that the provinces should be doing – health care and education and such – it is also doing less of what it should be doing: speaking as the nation's voice in foreign councils, advancing Canadian trade, managing immigration, forging closer regional ties through trade and travel. If we can't think of something for Ottawa to do, we could lose the country through lack of mandate

As the regions drift apart at the same time that power becomes ever more concentrated in the hands of party elites, political parties become more and more divorced from the electorate. In *Fights of Our Lives,* a book about epic Canadian elections, Liberal strategist and consultant John Duffy talks about the brokerage function of political parties. In earlier times, he observes, MPs and the regional party bosses served as conduits, sounding out the local citizens and relaying those concerns to the party leadership. Today, they serve that function less and less, in part because the parties themselves are effectively excluded from large portions of the country, and in part because party leaderships are content to rely on polls, focus groups, and other modern tools of taking the public's temperature. Those tools may be effective, but the organic connection between party and community is lost.

But there is a new grassroots – the Netroots of the web. Barack Obama captured the Democratic Party's nomination by forging an online alliance of previously disenfranchised and uninterested young voters and urban liberals, who were ultimately joined by African Americans and Latinos of all ages and incomes. After the election, the formidable email list was transferred to the Democratic National Committee, and the administration has stayed in direct contact with its supporters, urging them to gather at house parties to watch the latest video on health care or the economic stimulus package and to submit questions online. Headquarters staff answer many of those questions, encouraging a back-and-forth flow of information and advice.

Let's not be naive. The president of the United States doesn't spend his evenings reading emails from voters and checking Twitter for new tweets. Online interaction between the administration and Obama supporters might be nothing more than a con game, to keep the base onside and the donations flowing in. But it may also be more than that: it may be another form of communication between political elites and the people, a way of consulting with them, hearing their concerns. People did actually meet at economic-stimulus house parties. They did canvass in March in support of the budget. They will be tracking the stimulus money on www.recovery.gov as the billions flow from Washington to the rest of the country. The new administration and the people who put it in charge are talking and listening to each other.

Nothing exists like this in Canada. Partly this is because none of the leaders engages voters the way

Obama engaged his supporters. Partly it is because Canada is, as always, a few years behind the United States in adapting to new electoral techniques. But fundamentally it's because political parties here don't *think* the way they need to think. They don't see themselves as open, organic institutions talking and listening to a broad swath of Canadians. They talk only to their party faithful, and the faithful are few in number.

This has to change. "Why do you have to pay ten dollars to join a political party? Why should you have to join a political party at all, to vote for the leader?" John Duffy asked in a recent conversation. "What if you simply registered as a Conservative or Liberal voter, and that registration was sufficient to cast a ballot for party leader?"

Or what if membership were free and it were possible to take out a temporary membership, good only for the period of a leadership campaign? What if leadership votes were conducted online, so everyone could vote easily? What if votes were staggered, with different parts of the country voting at different times, so that Canadians in all parts of Canada could hear what Canadians in other parts of Canada were thinking?

Canada's Barack Obama — and she's out there, though she may be busy right now, studying for exams — will run for the leadership of a party that has opened itself to all interested voters, voters who galvanize around a candidate who excites them, who want to embrace her call for change and renewal, who endorse her plans to bring about that renewal, who organize themselves through Facebook and MySpace and Twitter, who create a political storm that sweeps away the wreckage of the old politics, the old animosities, the tired grievances of the past.

That will be the day that Canada enters the twenty-first century; that a new Canada begins to emerge; that our citizens, in conversation with each other, begin to forge a national identity that they create for themselves, rather than having others create it for them; and that finds its expression in a young, new, connected leadership. That will be the day when Valerie Chu decides she really could become prime minister.

Chapter 3

Yes, Mr. President; No, Prime Minister

WHAT COULD BE WORSE than electing judges? Everyone knows that requiring the judiciary to run for election and re-election in state-level courts is a terrible flaw in the American system. Incompetents get elected by promising to hang every shoplifter from a lamp post; powerful interests fund the campaigns of malleable justices; a lawyer donates money to a judge's campaign one day – or declines to – and then argues before that same judge the next. In March, the Supreme Court heard arguments in a case in which a state court judge ruled in favour of an energy company, throwing out a $50 million penalty, after the company's CEO spent $3 million to get the judge elected.

How vastly superior the Canadian system of appointed judges is; how grateful we should all be to the Fathers of Confederation for emulating the British rather than the American model.

Except we're not. A 2007 Strategic Counsel poll revealed that 63 per cent of Canadians would like to elect their judges too. According to a University of Chicago study in 2007, elected judges in the States perform as well as appointed judges. Americans would probably also elect their Supreme Court judges, if they were allowed to. And maybe they should be.

One of the more enduring myths, perpetuated mostly by members of the Canadian public service,[*] is that we have a tremendous advantage over the American political system because our bureaucrats are hired and promoted purely on the basis of merit, while theirs are appointed for political favours rendered. Just as Americans are irresponsible in electing judges, district attorneys, and dog catchers, goes the argument, so, too, they compromise their federal public service by allowing thousands of major appointments to be based on patronage. Partisan considerations infect

---

[*] In this chapter, "public service" refers to the core public administration – generally speaking, those public servants employed directly by the federal government, excluding the military, the RCMP, and semi-autonomous public agencies.

policy choices; priorities and approaches see-saw with each change of administration; men (mostly) whose only qualification is that they helped get a president elected are awarded with positions of power and prestige. Disgraceful.

Actually, it's our system that is closer to being a disgrace. Ours is a bureaucracy in decline, another blow to the health of the federal political culture, further proof that Ottawa is sick and getting sicker.

Canada's federal public service is old. According to a recent Statistics Canada report, 52 per cent of the core public service is over forty-five. In the general population, only 39 per cent of workers are over forty-five. The Canadian workforce overall is aging, but there are few workers older than a federal public servant at the peak of his career.

Not only is he old, he's white. Despite a slew of affirmative action programs, the public service is unable to attract and retain immigrants – the vast majority of whom now come from non-white home countries – or their children. Only 10 per cent of new hires in the federal public service belong to a visible minority, according to Statistics Canada, even though their share of the population is 16 per cent and is expected to reach 20 per cent in the next decade.

Don Oliver, a Nova Scotia senator, thinks the reason is racism."Look at the power structure," he told the *Hill Times* in January 2008. "The clerk is white. The deputy clerk is white. All of the deputy ministers are white. Most of the ADMs [assistant deputy ministers] are white." Visible minorities in the lower ranks of the service "just can't make it to the top because of these systemic racial barriers that keep visible minorities out of the power in the public service." He calls it "a disgraceful situation."

Senior public servants – all of them white, of course – would strongly deny any element of racism in their hiring decisions. They're both right and wrong. Any visible-minority Canadian who is comfortable with the culture and environment of the federal public service is welcome to join it. It probably doesn't even occur to those at the top that it is that very culture that pushes Canadians with an Indian, Chinese, or other non-European background away.

For one thing, to get very far up the ladder, you have to be bilingual. In one respect, that is as it should be. Canada is a bilingual country and its public service must speak to Canadians in both official languages. But the vast majority of Canada's immigrants speak English. French-language training is onerous, and proficiency cannot be guaranteed. For an IT graduate choosing between offers from the private and public sector, the hassle of acquiring French is just another reason to avoid Ottawa and take that job in Kitchener instead. The bilingual requirement effectively restricts the hiring pool for the management ranks of the federal public service to the so-called bilingual belt along or near the Ontario–Quebec and the Quebec–New Brunswick border. Not only does this limit the number of immigrants eligible to join, it effectively freezes out candidates from Western provinces. No wonder the West feels estranged from Ottawa. Few in the capital are from there.

There's another reason the brightest and best avoid joining the mandarinate. Several years ago, the Privy Council Office commissioned David Eaves, who today is a young specialist in negotiations and a policy analyst, and who was even younger then, to explore how the federal public could better network, leverage, and enable young public servants. Over lunch, he explained to me why his report would essentially tell the PCO that the situation was worse than imagined.

"How do you address Philip Crawley?" he asked. Crawley is the publisher of the *Globe and Mail*.

"I call him Philip," I replied.

"What does the clerk in the mail room call him?"

"He calls him Philip. Everyone calls him Philip."
Newsrooms are very informal places.

"If you needed to see Philip Crawley right away, could you?"

I shrugged. "Sure. Though it would have to be for a very good reason."

"Could the mail room clerk see him right away?"
David asked.

"Same thing," I replied. "If the clerk in the mail room thinks there is something that the publisher needs to hear about right away, the publisher will want to know what that is."

"Exactly," said Eaves. "The public service isn't like that."

Eaves believes, and there is plenty of evidence to suggest he's right, that his generation — especially knowledge workers, those whom the writer Richard Florida has dubbed the Creative Class — simply won't work in the structured, hierarchical environments common to bureaucracies. They don't do nine-to-five; they balk at writing a report that someone else then summarizes and presents to someone else, who may or may not pass the findings up the chain. They have been raised in a world of virtual social networks, instant messaging, texting. Why would they want to work in a place where everyone can't talk to everyone about anything? It's not that Eaves's generation is social-ist or anarchic: they understand how power flows within an organization. They just don't want to wear ties, and if they think they need to talk to the deputy minister, they want to be able to talk to the deputy min-ister. They don't do bureaucracy.

It is also unclear, Eaves added in a recent exchange, whether the public service truly is a meritocracy. "In a meritocracy, you can get rid of the deadwood and the underperformers," he explained. "In Canada's public service, it is virtually impossible to get rid of anyone," thanks to labour contracts and other protections.

As some departments become filled with under-performers, he said, the talent moves out, frustrated or bored. The only way to get rid of the incompetents might be to promote them. Every public servant knows it happens. "A perverse, inverse Peter Principle is at work," Eaves says. "Rather than getting promoted to their level of incompetence, often people are pro-moted beyond it."

All public services — and many private corpora-tions — struggle to overcome the rigidities and silos that inevitably develop in large, complex bodies. But the Canadian public service is particularly rigid, particularly resistant to change. One big reason is that the Canadian government doesn't have a Plum Book.

The Plum Book — the formal name is United States Government Policy and Supporting Positions — lists the 7,000 positions within the U.S. federal public service that can be filled without competitive examination. They include agency heads and their subordinates, policy advisers, and other senior officials. The president and his personal advisers directly appoint these coveted positions, though about 1,100 of them require Senate confirmation. Canadian mandarins tend to sniff at the process; it is patronage at its most rank. Public servants should rise to the top through merit, not because they helped deliver Indiana. If a career public servant, rather than Michael D. "you're-doing-a-heck-of-a-job-Brownie" Brown had been in charge of the Federal Emergency Management Agency when Hurricane Katrina struck, lives and property might have been saved, and the misery of thousands lessened.

Nonetheless, there are huge advantages to having the president appoint the senior ranks of the public service. For one thing, the president can ensure, to the extent he wants to, that women and ethnic minorities are properly represented. With each new incoming administration, associations representing women, African Americans, Latinos, Asians, gays, and other groups press the government to hire from among their ranks, going so far as to draw up lists of people from their communities and pushing those lists on the president and his advisers. Just as diversity is one factor – though not the only one – when a president chooses his cabinet, so, too, it influences hiring decisions throughout the senior ranks.

Canada, in this respect, is doubly cursed. The senior ranks of the public service hire the junior ranks, ensuring conformity despite protests of commitment to diversity. And because Canada is a parliamentary democracy, the prime minister must choose his cabinet from among his MPs, with an occasional senator thrown in – a much smaller and less diverse talent pool than is available to the American president.

There is another, even bigger, benefit to the American system. Things get done. Paul Frazer, a former Canadian public servant who now works as a consultant in Washington, thinks Canadians seriously misunderstand this crucial advantage of the Plum Book. "The president is able to send into each department and agency people he can trust," he explains, "who know his priorities and who are determined to carry them out. This is especially important with the Obama administration because the president clearly is moving on so many substantive issues at once. He has very little time to accomplish his agenda."

The Canadian system does acknowledge the advantages of appointments, because in a few key, highly important posts, the prime minister reserves the right to choose whomever he wants. The position of ambassador to the United States is arguably the most important in the Department of Foreign Affairs. The prime minister appoints the ambassador, usually a senior figure within the prime minister's party, as a message to the president that this representative can reach the PM at any time and that when he speaks, the PM is speaking.

The American president is able to inject that authority throughout the federal public service. Yes, public servants are expected to speak truth to power. But power resides within their own departments, in the plushest of corner offices. And power is there to see to it that the line officers of the department know the president's priorities and carry them out.

In Canada, the minister is very often not the most

important person in a department. After all, ministers come and go – lately, some departments, Foreign Affairs in particular, have had to install a revolving door. The deputy minister, who is the most important bureaucrat in each department, advises the minister, but reports to the clerk of the Privy Council, the boss of public-service bosses. If the minister and the deputy minister disagree, the deputy minister can simply do an end run and report his problem to the clerk, who can then hash it out with the prime minister, even though the minister might simply have been trying to implement the prime minister's wishes. This may help explain why American cabinet secretaries are more powerful than Canadian cabinet ministers – imagine an American president shuffling his cabinet – and why the most powerful nation on earth can make do with twenty members of cabinet, while the Canadian government currently can't get by with fewer than thirty-eight. The more powerful you are, the fewer there are like you.

The Plum Book provides another valuable – in fact, indispensible – service. It prevents the federal public service from ossifying. Every four – or, at the most, eight – years, an infusion of new leaders shakes up all government departments. They bring with them novel approaches and philosophies, preventing intellectual atrophy within the bureaucracy.

Critics complain that these patronage appointments disrupt planning, depress morale, and make for bad policy. There's truth in this. Line officers can become discouraged because political appointees invariably land the best jobs in their departments. And it can take months for a new administration to fill all Plum Book positions, leaving the department rudderless. When Obama's first choice for health secretary, Tom Daschle, had to drop out in February because of an embarrassment over taxes, it took until March for Obama to nominate a replacement, Kansas governor Kathleen Sebelius. And as March morphed into April, Treasury Secretary Tim Geithner struggled to rescue the banking sector and claw back bonuses from AIG executives without the aid of senior staff. In that sense, the American system is far from perfect. But the critics should look at the Canadian alternative.

Our federal public service is notoriously resistant to outside influences. Short-term appointments of experts from outside the public service to senior positions in it, to advise on policy or to help craft new programs, are discouraged. Nothing and no one is welcome who might disturb the collective mindset. As a result, Canada lacks the sorts of public-policy intellectuals who exercise so much influence within the United States. These uber-mandarins shuttle between government and universities, think-tanks and corporations, depending on who's in power and what's on offer.

The system produces people such as Condoleezza Rice, who taught at Stanford before being brought into the State Department of Bush the Elder, where she advised on Soviet policy, playing a key role in that administration's brilliant winding down of the Cold War. She returned to Stanford in 1991, joined the Hoover Institute and the board of Chevron Corporation (helping to negotiate a multibillion-dollar oil development with Kazakhstan, for which a grateful Chevron named a supertanker after her) before becoming the first woman, first minority, and youngest-ever provost at Stanford. George W. Bush brought her back to Washington, where she served as national security adviser and secretary of state before Obama's victory sent her back west.

On the Democratic side, take a look at another Rice, this one Susan. Like Condoleezza Rice, she is African American, but they are not related, and Susan

Rice, at forty-five, is a decade younger. A Stanford graduate and Rhodes Scholar with a D.Phil. from Oxford, Rice offered foreign policy advice to Michael Dukakis during his abortive run for president in 1988, then signed on at McKinsey, a management consulting company that some of us suspect runs the world, then joined the National Security Council when Clinton became president, rising to assistant secretary of state for African affairs. After the Republicans won in 2000, she briefly worked in the private sector before joining the Brookings Institution, a liberal think-tank. During the 2008 election, she advised Obama on foreign policy, and he, in turn, named her to cabinet as ambassador to the United Nations.

In Canada, all of this would be considered pork, patronage, one degree shy of corrupt, which is why there are no Rices, of either the Condoleezza or Susan variety, in the federal public service. When deputy ministers get together for a retreat, a group of old hands greet each other with the familiarity of comrades who have been in the trenches together for decades. They joined the public service out of university – may even have known each other in university, since a small coterie of central Canadian schools churns out most of the cohorts for the mandarinate. They rose through the ranks together, perhaps competed with one another for jobs, finally reaching the top of the bureau-cratic heap. Some of them may have been seconded to a job outside the federal public service for a year or two, but none of them has any of the diverse skills and experiences of their American counterparts. This band of brothers and sisters is charged with shaping foreign, financial, and trade policy, with regulation and coordination and standard-setting. Every now and then their political masters will tell them that they must re-engineer their department to make it more accountable, responsive, and relevant to a multicultural society and a twenty-first-century environment. How can they? They have little experience outside the insti-tution they're expected to reform. They have little knowledge of the society the rest of us live in.

Kevin Lynch, Clerk of the Privy Council, joined the Bank of Canada after earning a Ph.D. at McMaster. He transferred from there to the Finance department, moved over to Industry, ultimately becoming deputy minister, before returning as deputy minister of Finance. His sole experience outside the federal government consists of two years as Canada's repre-sentative at the International Monetary Fund. Any scan of the list of deputy ministers under his command reveals a similar pattern. These people are all skilled, intelligent, capable leaders. But they are monks, and Ottawa is their monastery. Who are they to Calgary, or Calgary to them? How could they possibly understand the way of the real world?

There's an ancillary benefit to the American rotation of people in and out of the senior ranks. As others have observed, it makes it much harder for the government to keep secrets. People who have read all the crucial documents and been at all the crucial meetings take that knowledge with them when they return to the academy or the private sector. People being people, they like to gossip, to show off how influential they were. Or they direct their students' research to certain areas, knowing that the students will eventually stumble onto a report the world should know about. That, Canadian public servants would retort, is the very reason we don't want people parachuting in and out of senior positions. Open. Closed.

Some would argue that provincial bureaucracies are no different. And Queen's Park, say, is hardly the nimblest of policy shops. But provincial public services generally do have a better track record of recruiting senior managers with private-sector or other real-world experiences. And because they are closer to their clients – both physically and in terms of the services, such as health care and education, that they provide – they tend to be less disconnected from what's happening on the ground than their counterparts in Ottawa. Which is another reason why, if you're young, smart, and ambitious and you want to work in government, the provinces may be the better bet.

There is a counterargument to this, and it has merit. The Canadian public service, like Canada itself, may be stodgy and resistant to change, but at least it's stable, with a long corporate memory and an impressive record of accomplishment. One example: for more than a decade, critics derided the hidebound regulations that prevented Canadian banks from diversifying their business so that they could successfully compete in the global market. I was one of those critics. Sorry about that.

As it turns out, those regulations prevented Canada's banks from gorging themselves on leveraged assets based on flim-flam mortgages, which fuelled a housing bubble such as the world has never seen before. Those brilliant public-policy intellectuals, brought into government by Bill Clinton and George W. Bush, pushed for and presided over the deregulation of the financial markets that made that bubble possible.

"Guess which country, alone in the industrialized world, has not faced a single bank failure, calls for bailouts or government intervention in the financial or mortgage sectors," wrote Fareed Zakaria in the February 16 issue of *Newsweek*. "Yup, it's Canada. In 2008, the World Economic Forum ranked Canada's banking system the healthiest in the world. America's ranked 40th, Britain's 44th." The TD Bank, he observed, has risen from being the fifteenth largest bank in North America a year ago to fifth largest today, simply because its competitors have collapsed.

Similarly, the Canadian housing market is far more stable than its American counterpart because the banks were allowed to lend mortgages only to people who could afford to repay them, and because Canadian tax law doesn't permit home owners to deduct mortgage interest from their income tax – an insane policy that costs the American treasury $100 billion, discourages American home owners from paying down their mortgages, and does nothing to encourage home own-ership, which is proportionately higher in Canada than in the United States. More than one febrile Canadian politician has proposed bringing mortgage-interest deductibility to Canada. The idea has always been shot down, largely because of the informed arguments coming out of the Department of Finance.

"If President Obama is looking for smart government, there is much he, and all of us, could learn from our quiet – OK, sometimes boring – neighbor to the north," Zakaria concluded.

Both bureaucratic cultures have their strengths. In Canada, policy flows both up and down, from the public service to government and from cabinet to the public service. Defenders of the Canadian system would also point out that there is a Plum Book of sorts here, in the form of the appointed staff who advise cabinet ministers, though they are fewer in number and far less powerful than the heavy hitters parachuted directly into the American bureaucracy.

But here's one way to gauge which of the two public services is more responsive and effective. Barack Obama's 2010 budget, the most groundbreaking of its kind since Ronald Reagan's first budget, will have to clear many hurdles in Congress. But if it passes in anything like its current form, and if Obama can get his Plum Book appointments filled, he will have a dedicated coterie of advocates in every department charged with creating the cap-and-trade system to lower greenhouse gas emissions; with expanding health care coverage, with modernizing schools and teaching methods. If an equally aggressive Canadian budget were foisted on the Canadian public service, could its policies be as swiftly implemented? Having watched both bureaucracies, my money would be on the Americans to get the job done. With all its faults, the Plum Book system is better at implementing change and regenerating a bureaucracy that, by its very nature, prefers stasis over reform.

Consider just one of Obama's proposed reforms: creating the cap-and-trade system to reduce carbon dioxide emissions. We don't know yet how successful the administration will be in getting the measure through Congress, but experience suggests that, if it passes, America will get a carbon market, for good or for ill. Canada was supposed to have one years ago. It's how this country was going to meet its Kyoto commitments to fight global warming. We made that commitment in 1997. We're still waiting.

Of course, political dithering as much as bureaucratic interference has made Canada delinquent in meeting its international environmental obligations. But that takes us to the heart of the problem. Chronic political instability has left the public service adrift.

Without direction, stability turns to stagnation. And stagnation is what we're increasingly seeing in the public service in Ottawa.

The worst, though not the only, example of decline can be found in Foreign Affairs – along with Finance and Defence, the most important responsibility of the federal government. Since 2001, seven cabinet ministers – John Manley, Bill Graham, Pierre Pettigrew, Peter MacKay, Maxime Bernier, David Emerson, and Lawrence Cannon – have held the portfolio. (All of them, by the way, are white men. The United States hasn't had one of those as secretary of state since Warren Christopher, in Bill Clinton's first administration.) Secretaries of state and foreign ministers around the world have become accustomed to the notion that the first time they meet a Canadian foreign minister will also probably be the last. Those meetings, in any case, are rare. Because of the instability of Parliament, foreign affairs or other ministers rarely leave the country. In international forums, it's the deputy minister or some chief assistant to the assistant chief who shows up. This gets noticed.

There are global issues on which Canada wants to have a say: on international trade, on climate change, even on the Middle East. But no one listens to Canada

anymore. And the constant rotation of cabinet ministers, coupled with the Harper government's obsession
with domestic policy as the key to its survival, makes it
impossible to develop a sustained, coherent approach
to these issues. In the larger sense, Canada no longer
has a foreign policy.

Our troops serve valiantly, and at great cost in
blood and to the treasury, in Afghanistan. But we have
no real voice in this latest version of the Great Game
and have declared our intention to abandon the
mission in 2011 in any case. We continue to insist that
the newly melting waters of the Arctic Archipelago
are within our jurisdiction, but have succeeded in
convincing nobody that that's the case. Arctic security
can be guaranteed only by the American military;
Canada just refuses to accept this truth. Our policy
on China is to insult them on both human rights and
Taiwan and then implore them to buy things from us.
Stephen Harper's sudden decision to bolster relations
with South America and the Caribbean is intriguing
but capricious and contradicts a parallel priority: to
exclude Mexico from discussions with the U.S. on
border issues, something we'll talk more about in the
next chapter.

When Congress debated President Obama's

economic stimulus package, Canada joined the chorus of nations protesting its Buy American provisions, which could prevent corporations based here from bidding on projects funded with stimulus money. Obama has promised that the United States will abide by its international trade commitments, but lawyers exist to make those commitments mean whatever the United States wants them to mean. In any case, by the time any complaint is adjudicated, the money will long since have been disbursed.

Ottawa seems to have forgotten that our lists of complaints change little or nothing in Washington. America is a trading nation, and it trades in foreign policy as well. If there's something you want from them, you have to offer something in return. We'll get to that as well in the next chapter, but the fundamental truth is that the men and women at the Lester B. Pearson Building, the home of Foreign Affairs in Ottawa, largely confine themselves to threat analysis and response.

And they're not always very good at that. Many commentators warned Ottawa as far back as 2004 that Congress was serious about closing America's borders to anyone without a passport, including Canadians. Won't happen, scoffed those in the know at Fort

Pearson and the PMO. It's an unfunded mandate. They'll never pay what it would cost to implement the system. When it became clear that they did have the will and the means, the Canadian side fought for delay. Passports are now mandatory for air travel and go into effect at land crossings in June. Some unfunded mandate.

There are still plenty of skilled and dedicated officers doing their best to protect Canada's interests and contribute to the global conversation. But they are being undermined by events and by politicians who have lost control over those events. The great department that St. Laurent led – and Pearson, and Clark, and Axworthy, and Manley – is falling apart.

Some critics might respond that foreign affairs is being centralized in governments around the world, that the State Department isn't what it used to be either, nor the British Foreign Office, nor the Quai d'Orsay. Perhaps. But Hillary Clinton and the people who work for her play a far greater role in shaping American foreign policy than this month's foreign affairs minister plays in shaping Canada's.

And there's a larger point. Foreign Affairs is not *the* big, dysfunctional department in Ottawa. It is one of many big, dysfunctional departments. I've already mentioned the embarrassing mess that Environment Canada and other departments made of (not) implementing Kyoto. I could leave you rolling in the aisles with stories about the bungled gun registry. The Finance department's abrupt reversal on the question of income trusts enraged investors who rightly believed that the least they were entitled to in Canadian tax policy was coherence. The federal government seems fundamentally incapable of getting a new copyright act passed, despite years of talk and effort. During the time that I was political affairs columnist at the *Globe,* on slow days I would update readers on the tortuous attempts by successive Parliaments to pass laws toughening the penalties for animal cruelty and for creating a do-not-call list to deter telemarketers. Last year, the animal-cruelty legislation finally made it through Parliament, though it had been so watered down that observers described the changes as practically worthless. As for the do-not-call list, it was up and running last September, a mere two years after the bill passed. But people are complaining that they are getting more calls than ever. Not only is the ban riddled with exemptions, any telemarketer – including offshore firms not bound by Canadian law – can easily get hold of the list. Turns out it's a great marketing tool.

Worst of all, the federal public service has presided over the catastrophic mismanagement of Native policy. Under Ottawa's tender mercies, generation after generation of Indians, Métis, Inuit, and non-status Aboriginals have languished in poverty, deprived of proper education, adequate housing, decent health care, or any meaningful hope for a better future. It is Canada's shame, and Ottawa bears much of the blame.

The media, and the public they represent, must take some responsibility for this delinquency. A modern public service should be flexible, able to cut across departmental lines, its managers exercising responsibility without constantly having to go up the chain of command for approval. But every time the Privy Council Office tries to implement reform, someone makes a bad decision, the press gets wind of it, enraged opposition leaders flay the minister responsible, and new, more restrictive, rules are applied. Politics is more often than not the enemy of policy, and the press makes sure that the former paralyzes the latter.

The sponsorship scandal in Quebec provided the most recent and egregious example. Yes, there was corruption in the Department of Public Works. In the wake of the 1995 referendum, money poured into

Quebec to promote Canada at sporting events, trade shows, and the like. A corrupt bureaucrat, Chuck Guité, and some crooked advertising executives colluded to siphon money from the program, some of which got kicked back to the Liberal Party. Despite years of audits, reports, and the Gomery inquiry, there is no evidence the wrongdoing in Ottawa went any higher than Guité. The Gomery report led to tight new reporting restrictions in each department. And the Harper Tories, who rode to power on the scandal and the disgust it generated among voters, have restricted bureaucratic freedom of action still further. It's hard, sometimes, to dispute the allegation that Stephen Harper sees the public service as his personal enemy. No wonder just about nothing gets done.

Despite the mediocrity and ineffectiveness of our political class and our public service, Canada carries on. People get to work, the young learn in school, the sick are treated, new immigrants arrive, our troops hold the line. The failures are calculated as chances missed, directions not taken, opportunities passed by.

But failures can also cause harm, can cost people their jobs, can threaten the country's future. One big failure stretches from the western extremity of our country to its eastern. The situation is serious and getting slowly worse. If we don't wake up and act, it could cost you your job, it could make us a poorer and more fragile country.

It's south of you. It's the border.

Chapter 4

The Shutting of the Open Border

ON FEBRUARY 4, I wrote a column for the *Globe and Mail* excoriating the sorry state of the Department of Foreign Affairs. The next day, someone who knows that shop intimately phoned. The caller said the article overlooked that fact that the full name of the department is Foreign Affairs and International Trade, and on the trade side, the track record was much better. The Harper government had successfully negotiated a resolution to the chronic softwood lumber dispute, and earlier, the Martin government had navigated the mad cow scare while protecting the Canadian beef industry. In recent months, Canada has signed free trade agreements with Iceland, Norway, Switzerland, and Liechtenstein (known as the European Free Trade Area), Colombia, and Peru. To the extent that foreign policy is trade policy, the caller said, Canada is doing all right.

Point taken. (Though new trade agreements with the European Union, China, and India would be much more impressive accomplishments.) But on the trade issue that matters above all others, the future of our trading relationship with the United States, a succession of governments has failed to detect and overcome a steady deterioration in the flow of goods, services, and people. And that was before Canada was confronted with the threat of Barack Obama.

The new American president travelled briefly to Canada on February 19, 2009, his first foreign visit as president. There are plenty of connections between Obama and Canada: his half-sister, Maya Soetoro-Ng, is married to a Chinese-Canadian doctor, though the couple now lives in Hawaii; David Axelrod, Obama's chief strategist, once advised Dalton McGuinty when he was Opposition leader in Ontario; there are connections between senior Obama officials and Michael Ignatieff, from the Liberal leader's days teaching at Harvard, though this can hardly comfort Stephen Harper. Nonetheless, the meeting between the president and the prime minister went well by all accounts, ending with an anodyne agreement to co-operate in protecting trade flows while working to improve the environment. About what you'd expect from a brief courtesy visit.

Canadians adore Barack Obama. In one poll last year, 15 per cent of them said they would give up the right to vote in the Canadian election if they could vote in the American one. It's a safe bet that almost all of them would have voted for Obama. He's the multi-cultural Canadian prime minister that Canada has never had, embodying our values of diversity better than the vast majority of Canadian politicians. Besides, he's the coolest guy on the planet. His favourable rating in Canadian polls is above 80 per cent, an astonishing figure for any political leader.

Yet Canadians may well be ignoring their own self-interest in supporting Obama. For decades, Canada has flourished in an ever-more-globalized world. But Barack Obama may be about to bring that world to an end. He is the first postglobal president.

In July 1944, at Bretton Woods, the Allied nations committed the world to freer trade. The wealth that more open borders generated around the world in the postwar years encouraged governments everywhere to go further. Advances in communications technology and fresh commitments to lower tariff barriers made it possible for capital to flow as freely as goods. Globalization, as these flows came to be called, unleashed enormous economic potential, lifting billions of people in East and South Asia out of poverty. As a recent *Economist* article reported, the size of the middle class (those who have a third of their income left over after paying for shelter and other basic necessities) in the Third World increased from one-third of the population in 1990 to one-half today. "The developing world is no longer simply poor," the magazine observed.

The 1988 Canada–U.S. Free Trade Agreement and the 1993 North American Free Trade Agreement eliminated most of whatever tariffs remained between the two countries. Since the deals were signed, exports as a percentage of Canada's gross domestic product have doubled, from 25 per cent to 50 per cent. A country whose industry once consisted largely of branch plants has given the world the BlackBerry and Bombardier jets. With its small, scattered population and an economy based on natural resources, manufacturing, and financial services, it was and remains in Canada's interests to promote an ever-more globalized world.

But Barack Obama believes this growth has gone too far. As wide-open capitalism swept the globe, jobs drained away from American factories to sweatshops overseas, turning the entire industrial heartland of America into a Bruce Springsteen song. Gigantic pools of capital sloshed around the world, as governments recklessly dismantled their regulatory regimes and Masters of the Universe gamed whatever was left of the system to accumulate staggering personal wealth, even as middle- and working-class incomes stagnated or declined. Everyone, everywhere, took on too much debt, with lenders offering and buyers accepting mortgages that both sides knew could never be supported, and with everyone counting on ever-rising housing prices to somehow make it all right, until finally the whole global Ponzi scheme came crashing down, smashing the financial sector, freezing credit, throwing millions out of work, deflating prices, and leaving the planet's economy teetering on the edge of a new Depression.

This is the America-in-the-world that Barack Obama inherited, and it is a world he aims to remake, starting at home. The almost $800 billion stimulus package he signed on February 17, and the 2010 budget proposal that followed a week later were not simply bold, if desperate, efforts to replace private demand with public, in order to weaken and ultimately reverse the recession; their main tenets were also the foundation for a new economic and social order, a postglobal America that Obama envisioned long before the crash afforded him the opportunity to accelerate his agenda.

In this America, individuals will re-engage with their communities through relationships based on mutual responsibility and consideration, the legacy of Obama's years as a community organizer. Washington will become more active in educating the young, providing access to health care, and renewing the national infrastructure. The federal government will also become a diligent custodian of the environment, substantially reducing pollution and greenhouse gases through enlightened environmental and energy policies. All of this will be financed through a more progressive form of taxation that asks the rich to contribute their fair share, coupled with the elimination of programs, such as some agricultural subsidies, that have outlived their usefulness. Meanwhile, regulators will keep a watchful eye on Wall Street to prevent future outrages of capitalism, in an economic system that places greater emphasis on work for workers than on capital for investors. In such an America, limited protectionism is acceptable if it preserves economic sovereignty and the fruits of labour. This is Barack Obama's America.

"What is required of us now is a new era of responsibility," he said in his inaugural address, "a recognition, on the part of every American, that we have duties to ourselves, our nation and the world; duties that we do not grudgingly accept but rather seize gladly, firm in the knowledge that there is nothing so satisfying to the spirit, so defining of our character, than giving our all to a difficult task.

"This is the price and the promise of citizenship."

There are those among us, including me, who question whether this postglobal America is feasible or desirable. The Pollyanna optimism that fossil fuels can be easily and swiftly displaced by green alternatives could lead to the worst of all possible worlds: an increased reliance on coal and imported oil, as new-technology experiments fizzle and more feasible alternatives (such as nuclear energy) are neglected. Even if, as Obama promises, renewable energy output doubles over the next three years, that will still only represent 12 per cent of consumption, with fossil and nuclear fuels responsible for most of the rest. Poverty overseas could worsen, while growth at home remains sluggish or worse, as an overregulated economy chokes capital investment and political calculation undermines market forces. The postglobal future may not be anything more than a return to the 1970s.

But the new president believes otherwise, and he is nothing if not confident and decisive. First came executive orders. California, followed by at least seventeen other states, including Florida, wanted (even before Obama took office) to pass new laws that would require automakers to reduce by 2016 the greenhouse gas emissions of their cars by 30 per cent. George Bush ordered the Environmental Protection Agency to veto the request; Obama ordered the EPA to reconsider. Under its new, Democrat-appointed leadership, the agency is expected to give California and other states the green light, and soon. Obama backed up that order with another, mandating a fleet-wide standard of thirty-five miles per gallon by 2020.

"The days of Washington dragging its heels are over," he declared. Seems like he means it.

As the economic crisis worsened, the new president heaped biblical condemnation on Wall Street executives who had paid themselves billions in bonuses even as their tottering banks held their hands out for government money to forestall bankruptcy. Most emphatically, Obama signed without qualm the massive economic stimulus legislation, worth almost $800 billion, which includes the notorious Buy American provisions. While in Ottawa, Obama assured Harper that he remained committed to protecting an open trading system. There's no reason not to believe him. The president is an intelligent man who reads his history, and he knows that in the 1930s rising protectionism in the United States led to a global collapse of trade that worsened the Great Depression. His economic advisers are all committed free traders.

But the Buy American provisions, however they are implemented, reflect a greater problem. Even before Obama's arrival, the state of Canada–U.S. relations could best have been described as quietly troubled. Granted there are no crises, no softwood lumber or mad-cow disputes, currently on the agenda. But relations between the two countries are strained on several fronts. Barack Obama's agenda, to the extent he is truly determined to implement it, will worsen that strain. If he's not careful, he could break something.

The president's commendable concern for the environment directly threatens the Canadian economy.

Extracting oil from the sticky bitumen of Alberta's oil sands generates three times the greenhouse gas emissions of conventional drilling. For George W. Bush, whose chief concern was security of supply, that mattered not one whit. But environmentalists are pressing Obama to limit imports of dirty Canadian oil. Obama, in response, talks vaguely about using carbon-capture technology to lessen the environmental impact of both oil- and coal-generated power. But carbon sequestration technology – burying captured carbon dioxide underground so it doesn't escape into the atmosphere – is hugely expensive and largely unproven. Nonetheless, the president appears determined to wean America off its dependence on fossil fuels, and his pledge to Congress to move forward on instituting a cap-and-trade system to reduce greenhouse gas emissions will also make Alberta's dirty oil less appealing.

The only thing that could conceivably matter more to Obama than rescuing the environment is protecting the jobs of upper Midwestern blue-collar voters. He owes his presidency to them. The Democrats are on the cusp of what could be a generational lock on power. In 2008, the Republican base was reduced to the Deep South, the Bible Belt, and the Great Plains states. These voters are white, poor, and aging. As Republicans in Congress cater to this base, they alienate the party from the broader electorate; Sarah Palin and Rush Limbaugh are the pied pipers who could lead the GOP over a cliff.

But the coalition of the young, urban liberals, African Americans, and Latinos isn't enough to guarantee the Democrats victory either. American elections hinge on the crucial swing votes of the industrial Midwest: the belt of states from Illinois to Pennsylvania. Voters there are largely lower income, blue collar, unionized, and socially conservative. They voted for Ronald Reagan and Bill Clinton. In 2008, economic fear drove them to the Democrats.

They remain the uncertain swing element of the Democratic coalition. If they come to believe that Obama has abandoned them, that he isn't really willing to fight to save their jobs, that he cares more about saving the upper atmosphere than saving them, that he is in thrall to liberal interests, just as Bush was in thrall to Wall Street, then they could abandon him, swing back to the Republicans, and put an end to the Obama presidency after one ignominious term. They are why Obama vowed during the primary campaign that he would force Mexico and Canada to renegotiate NAFTA or else he would withdraw the United States from it. By the time of his Canadian trip in February, the president had soft-pedalled his message; now he simply wants the environmental and labour accords attached to the treaty to be embedded within it, so that they will have greater legal weight. But any reopening of NAFTA, no matter how benignly motivated, would put the whole treaty in play, making it a tempting target for any number of protectionist-minded senators seeking favour with local farmers or manufacturers.

So we have a postglobal leader determined to save both the planet and Pittsburgh, in league with a Democratic Congress that has already revealed, through the Buy American provisions, a strongly protectionist stripe, with both committed to producing cleaner energy and protecting American jobs, especially manufacturing jobs in the upper Midwest. The combination couldn't be more threatening to Canada's trade prospects.

To talk about trade is to talk about the border. The Canada–U.S. trading relationship, the largest and most complex in the world, relies on a porous perimeter across which products move swiftly and easily. As Michael Kergin, a former Canadian ambassador to Washington, likes to say, Canada and the United States don't trade with each other; we make things together. A piston in a car's engine will cross the border four times while the car is being constructed. Three million Canadian and seven million American jobs depend on the $1.5 billion worth of trade that crosses the border each day.

But since the September 11 attacks, the border has steadily thickened, as the Americans demand more thorough and complex inspections of all types of vehicles. Wait times at the Fort Erie–Buffalo Peace Bridge are up a third since September 11, according to a 2007 Canadian Chamber of Commerce report; at Windsor–Detroit, they've nearly doubled. With wait times as long as three hours not uncommon, the Ontario government has had to install portable toilets along Highway 402 for cross-border travellers who've drunk too much coffee. The worsening delays, accompanied by new fees and charges imposed by the Americans, have created a new tariff-in-all-but-name, increasing the reluctance of American firms to site their operations in Canada. Commercial and passenger traffic at Ontario border crossings was down 4 per cent between 2006 and 2007.

With the arrival of the Obama administration, Canadian border watchers dared to hope that American paranoia about the security of their northern border might start to wane. Instead, within days of her confirmation as director of homeland security, Janet Napolitano ordered an urgent, multi-agency review of the northern border.

The review has dismayed Canadian officials at both the federal and provincial levels. During the Bush administration, Homeland Security effectively hijacked Canada–U.S. relations, shunting the State Department to the side. The gargantuan new department, charged with, among other things, protecting the nation's borders in the wake of the September 11 attacks, is innately suspicious of Canada. In April 2008, I was chatting amiably at a party with a very pleasant woman when her husband arrived, a bit the worse for drink. This being Washington, we promptly swapped business cards. He was a lawyer in the Department of Homeland Security. When he saw that I was a reporter with the *Globe and Mail,* he scowled. "You Canadians. You let in a whole lot of people and you don't know who they are." Unfortunately, he was simply reflecting the mindset of the department.

In 2007, Canada and the United States were set to launch a pilot project for customs preclearance. In essence, the project would locate commercial customs clearance away from border crossings that have become chokepoints to secure facilities inland. Vehicles would be inspected, sealed if necessary, and allowed to cross the border without further inspection. Both sides had agreed that the first preclearance centre would be built at Fort Erie, to manage the Peace Bridge crossing. But in April 2007, Homeland Security vetoed the project. The General Accounting Office explained why in a report it released in November 2008.

The report stated that Canadian and American officials couldn't agree on the following issues: "arrest authority; the right of individuals to withdraw an application to enter the United States while at the land preclearance site in Canada; mutually agreeable fingerprinting processes; how information collected by U.S. officials at the land preclearance site would be shared; and concerns that future interpretations of the Canadian Charter could adversely impact U.S. authorities at the preclearance site."

In other words, they didn't trust us.

With the arrival of the Obama administration, there were high hopes on the Canadian side that

Homeland Security would be reined in and the two countries could work co-operatively to ease congestion at the border. Napolitano's review, and the fact that the first of several planned unmanned drone airplanes was deployed in February by the United States to monitor the North Dakota–Manitoba section of the border, suggests that the Americans are still concerned that we let in too many people and we don't know who they are.

Since the end of the Second World War, Canada has repeatedly acted boldly to protect and expand its trading relationship with the United States and the world. For more than thirty years, the Americans refused numerous Canadian proposals to proceed with a Great Lakes canal system for large vessels, bowing to pressure from the railways and the northeastern states, which rightly feared they would lose business. But when the St. Laurent government informed President Dwight Eisenhower that Canada was ready to proceed with an all-Canadian canal, the American president put the weight of his administration behind getting Congress to support a joint project, and in 1954, construction of the St. Lawrence

Seaway was underway. A decade later, Canadian nego-
tiator Simon Reisman led the team that proposed
the Auto Pact, which lowered Canadian tariffs on
U.S.–made automobiles in exchange for a guaranteed
share of production. The deal galvanized auto
production, so that today Ontario produces more
automobiles than Michigan. And it was Brian
Mulroney who proposed to Ronald Reagan that the
two countries negotiate the Canada–United States
Free Trade Agreement (though, according to some
accounts, Reagan let it be known that he wanted to
be asked).

The entire Canadian economy depends on free
trade with the United States. Our country simply
cannot allow the border to thicken further. The time
has come for the St. Lawrence Seaway, Auto Pact, and
NAFTA of our generation. The time has come – in
fact, we are overdue – for a North American
Environmental, Economic, and Security Accord.

Canada and the United States are well down the
path to a continental carbon market based on capping
industrial emissions and trading credits between busi-
nesses that are above or below their cap. Now that may
come as a surprise to you: after all, the United States
did not ratify the Kyoto agreement on reducing

greenhouse gases, and Canada conspicuously failed to meet its obligations under the treaty. But while both national governments were unwilling or unable to take action on climate change, states and provinces acted on their own. On the Eastern Seaboard, the Regional Greenhouse Gas Initiative, now embracing ten states led by New York, was up and running on January 1, 2009, targeting the power sector. Launched in 2007, the Western Climate Initiative (WCI) – encompassing seven Western states led by California, and also including Ontario, Quebec, British Columbia, and Manitoba – is not far behind. Even the six states of the coal-fired industrial Midwest, along with Manitoba, are moving on the Midwestern Greenhouse Gas Reduction Initiative, which has a proposed start-up date of 2012.

At their Ottawa get-together, Harper and Obama agreed to begin a senior-level "clean energy dialogue." And Environment Minister Jim Prentice pounded the halls of Congress in March, attempting to convince the Americans that both countries could work to reduce global warming without affecting oil sands production. But we should do more than talk. The two senior governments need to harmonize and expand these state and provincial initiatives in a single North American Climate Initiative, which would create a continental cap-and-trade system to meet common emission-reduction goals and set tough benchmarks for reducing smog-related contaminants. After all, breezes blow.

In his first address before Congress, Obama invited it "to send me legislation that places a market-based cap on carbon pollution and drives the production of more renewable energy in America." Maybe Canada should send him one as well. Any bilateral cap-and-trade agreement will offend industries and workers dependent on dirty oil-sands oil and dirtier American coal. We could partner with the United States to fund more aggressively research in carbon sequestration and other technologies for making hydrocarbon-based fuels cleaner, while accepting that the payoff for this research could take years. In exchange for this funding, of which the Americans would pay the lion's share, we should guarantee that 100 per cent of any oil extracted from the oil sands will be sold to the United States. This is a bargain for us. After all, it's not as though we were planning to build a pipeline to the Pacific.

Canadians need to understand, and it is the job of our political leaders to convince them, that, just as free trade in the 1980s and 1990s did nothing to lessen Canadian sovereignty or independence, so, too, a bilateral, continental security perimeter would make the continent safer for both Canadians and Americans without betraying our independence. The way to get the Americans to trust the border is to give them confidence that both countries have the will and ability to protect it. The security leg of this agreement, then, would include common rules for accepting refugees, joint inspection of containers leaving international destinations en route to either country, and an integrated terrorist watch list. Most important, it would expand NORAD, the joint command that protects the continent's airspace, to include land and water. This would lead to the presence of American forces on Canadian soil and within Canadian coastal waters. It would also lead to the presence of our forces on their territory. There's no reason to assume that either country's sovereignty would be compromised in the process.

Offering to move from co-operation to integration on security would afford Canada the opportunity to ask for the same on the economy. As the final tranche of this comprehensive continental agreement, Canada should propose a customs union.

This would be the biggest, boldest move Canada

could make: a joint tariff, based on bilateral consent, that would allow both countries to erase the border completely, permitting the free flow of goods, services, and people between our two countries, no passport or work visa required – a freedom those in the European Union already enjoy. As part of the union, both countries would drop all remaining protections in agriculture, cultural industries, and financial services. After all, our supply management boards are anachronisms, promoting inefficient farming and expensive milk in the nostalgic desire to preserve family farms that mostly no longer exist. Our artists are globally competitive – how would Americans laugh without our comedians, and where would bad popular music be without our Brian Adams, Céline Dion, and Shania Twain? – and in a world where information flows in every direction via the Internet, protecting such antiquities as television broadcasters and book, magazine, or newspaper publishers is as nonsensical as protecting the family farm. A customs union won't cost us our identity, whatever that is; it will produce the opposite. Just as NAFTA spurred Canadian business entrepreneurship, so, too, will dropping cultural protections encourage Canada's artistic entrepreneurs. The worst that will happen is that we may have to adopt American spelling.

As for protecting financial services, TD already has more branches in the United States than in Canada. If anything, the Americans should be demanding protection from us.

And no, this won't give Americans control over our immigration policy. For one thing, if they had any say over who we let in and how many, we would have some say over who and how many they let in. That wouldn't be such a bad thing: America's immigration system is littered with confusing categories and places too little emphasis on bringing in skilled workers. Instead, millions of Mexican and other Latinos flood the country, providing labour for jobs Americans aren't willing to do themselves. The Yanks could do worse than imitating us on immigration. But that's beside the point. What matters is that both countries would want to retain full control over their immigration policies, but that under the agreement each would welcome the other's citizens into its labour market. Canada would have to take steps to ensure that illegal immigrants don't move into Canadian jobs, but legality is already easy to verify.

But there's a caveat: if I'm wrong, if the Americans

would not agree to any further substantial easing of the border without significant restrictions on Canadian immigration, then Canada should walk away from the discussions. The only thing more important than promoting increased access to American markets is preserving Canada's robust multicultural identity. That identity is based on the world's most enlightened immigration policy, which encourages more people to move to our country, per capita, than any other nation, and which ensures that they come from all parts of the world, preventing the emergence of a race-based underclass such as the United States already created through slavery and is recreating through Latino immigration and which Europe is duplicating by allowing the vast majority of its immigrants to come from former colonies, which in many cases means northern Africa and the Middle East. Immigration is who we are. It is our future. It is the one thing we must never bargain away.

For the foreseeable future, any conversations we have with the United States over the border should not include Mexico. In this respect, NAFTA may actually have harmed the Canada–U.S. relationship. Every time Canada brings a border proposal to the United States, the Americans shake their head. "We'd be interested," they say, "but if we did it for you, we'd have to do it for the Mexicans." The truth is, Canada and the United States are developed nations, winners in the global lottery of wealth. Mexico, sadly, is not. As the frightening violence surrounding the drug cartels illustrates, the country is still far distant from becoming a modern, liberal democracy with a developed economy and adherence to the rule of law. Canada and the United States need to talk about the problems at our border. The Mexicans and the Americans can talk about their border on their own. That's why our border should be subject to a new treaty, not to NAFTA.

We live in the real world. Politically, a full environmental, security, and economic union is a proposal too far. But Stephen Harper should start with this level of proposed integration and then remove each item that is politically impossible until he reaches a package that he believes he can sell to his caucus, Parliament, and the Canadian public. And he should invite Michael Ignatieff to 24 Sussex for dinner, to explain that package. After all, the leader of the Opposition spent a considerable portion of his adulthood in the United States. If anyone understands the importance of improving the state of Canada–U.S. relations, it's Ignatieff. Let the opposition to the initiative align behind the Bloc, the NDP, and the Greens. Let's have an open debate on the proposal. Heck, let's have an election on it. We're having them all the time anyway. Why not fight one on something that actually matters?

And let us take this proposal to President Obama and tell him that in a postglobal world, this is what the relationship between Canada and the United States should be: two sovereign nations trading freely together, their citizens travelling back and forth between each other's countries, watching each other's backs, and working together to heal and protect the planet. This is what North America should be. This is what the world should be.

There are those who believe that the United States is an ailing giant, an empire in decline, and that the last thing Canada should do is bind itself to this collapsing colossus. They hold that Canada's economic future lies in diversifying our trading relationships. "The American century is over," my colleague Lawrence Martin wrote in the *Globe* in February. " . . . We will be forced, whether we like it nor not, to find other pastures."

Those other pastures could include China and India, the Asian behemoths that could overtake the United States in economic size sooner rather than later. It could include a free trade agreement with the European Union, a market that is already larger than America's and is growing in wealth as Eastern Europe shakes off the legacy of the Soviet occupation. It could include other emerging powerhouses, such as Brazil or even South Africa.

Such arguments are both right and ridiculous. Of course Canada should be diversifying its trading relationships. Actually, we already are. The share of goods flowing into the United States declined from 30 per cent of gross domestic product in 2000 to 21 per cent in 2007. Partly that's due to the thickening border, but mostly it's due to increased demand for commodities and manufactured goods from China and Europe.

But there are limits. China manipulates its currency to make it easy to export its products and to make it hard for anyone to export to its market. This is a chronic complaint among all countries who would like to increase trade with China. Canada will get improved access to the Middle Kingdom if and when the United States and the European Union convince or compel China to stop manipulating its currency. Our policy here can only be to keep our fingers crossed.

Similarly, it's hard to imagine the European Union negotiating a treaty with Canada that permits the unfettered access of our goods and services to, say, France. Germany will always have a closer relationship with France than Canada has. Sure, we have lots we could sell them, but most of it you cut down or dig up, and they're already buying that from us. What else do we have to offer to them, other than the ubiquitous BlackBerry and maybe a Bombardier jet or two? Do you really think they'd want our cars? Our chardonnay?

Finally, to those who want us to put our eggs in other baskets, please explain how you plan to protect those eggs. Critics of NAFTA rage that the treaty is unfair because the Americans violate it at whim and nothing in the agreement permits effective redress. It's true that both the Americans and the Canadians sin on NAFTA from time to time, though trade disputes represent a tiny fraction of the overall relationship. But do these critics actually believe that the Indians or the Russians are more to be trusted, that trade disputes with alternative markets won't arise, and that if they do, the World Trade Organization can be expected to protect Canadian interests? Which would you rather count on: direct talks between Canadians and Americans to resolve a trade dispute or an appeal to the WTO to settle a claim of fresh protectionist measures from Brazil?

Those who advocate lessening our reliance on trade with the United States and increasing our ties with countries overseas must answer one question: How? How are we to diversify our economy and reduce dependence on the American market in a way that places us in a position of competitive advantage over other nations seeking to enter those same new markets, and in a way that protects Canadian interests and jobs?

Actually, there's another question: Are you quite sure that these arguments for diversification aren't really just another manifestation of the visceral anti-Americanism that has infected some elements of Canadian society since the first Loyalists arrived? Aren't you arguing that America is in decline because you *want* it to be in decline? Haven't you made this argument many times before? Weren't you always wrong then? Are you sure you aren't wrong now?

———

When Canadians look to our southern border, we think of trade. When Americans look to their northern border, they think of security. The great challenge for our political leadership is to get Americans to look at the border with our eyes, and to get Canadians to see the border through theirs. If Canada and the United States cannot protect the environment together, if they cannot defend themselves from attack together, if they cannot work and live together, side by side, then what kind of future awaits us, post-global or otherwise?

And if greater integration is politically impossible, if our Parliament has become so chronically unstable and our bureaucracy so permanently sclerotic that nothing big can get done, nothing bold can even be proposed and debated on the floor of the House of Commons and in the offices and homes of the nation, then what is our future?

But I think we have it in us to reach agreement among ourselves and with the Americans on a new, open relationship for the twenty-first century. All we need are leaders willing to lead. Honestly, in the great sweep of things, it's not that far to go. We just have to get started.

Why don't we?

Chapter 5

Sundry Misconceptions

DURING THE YEARS OF George W. Bush's presidency, America's standing in the world plumbed the depths, and no wonder. It's not every day you get a U.S. administration that tortures people. Many non-Americans can't understand how George W. Bush got elected in the first place, let alone re-elected. They forget that the first time more people voted against him than voted for him. They forget as well – or simply could never understand, because they weren't there when it happened – the trauma that the attacks on New York and Washington inflicted on the American psyche. Al Qaeda's triumph left Americans angry and fearful in a way they hadn't been since Pearl Harbor. In the 2004 election, most of them simply didn't trust John Kerry, the Democratic presidential nominee, to keep them safe and extricate them from Iraq without leaving the place in an even worse state. But by 2006, in the wake of Hurricane Katrina and Abu Ghraib, they'd had enough. For the next two years, Bush was a dead president serving. The election of Barack Obama was America picking itself up, dusting itself off, and setting out again on its unique journey, though buffeted by the headwinds of an economic crisis.

What Canadians and others misunderstand about the United States is that it is constantly in flux; things there are always getting worse or better. You may think you understand some aspect of American culture, but your thinking is probably already out of date. You think America is a violent society with harsh laws? Crime rates are steadily falling, two-thirds of all Americans don't own a gun, and most Americans live in states that either ban or have placed a moratorium on capital punishment. You think Americans are more intolerant toward homosexuals than their counterparts elsewhere in the developed world? Massachusetts and Connecticut allow gay marriage, and California may soon join them. (The state already permits the equivalent of civil unions, so even if the courts uphold Proposition 8, which banned gay marriage, the civil rights of same-sex couples will still be protected.)

Washington, Oregon, New Jersey, New Hampshire, Maine, Hawaii, and the District of Columbia allow same-sex civil unions. All in all, almost a quarter of the American population live in states that protect the rights of gay partners. New York is expected to be next. You think America is racially divided? The cabinet of George W. Bush was the most diverse in American history, and the administration of Barack Obama is more diverse still. Compare that to the largely white, male uniformity of Canadian and European cabinets. You think the Americans are environmentally obtuse gluttons? Then why are Canadian provinces joining American state initiatives to combat global warming, in the absence of any effective national plan?

Casual aspersions about the dysfunctionality of American society blind its critics to the dynamic evolution constantly in play. Assumptions that America is in perpetual moral and social decline are not only insufferable, they are almost invariably wrong and out of date. And they blinker Canadians to a truth that we would rather not face. Our conservatism leads us to protect and defend what we should be changing, even as the United States no sooner achieves a status quo than it begins to dismantle it. America is forever moving on, while we too often stand still. This chapter looks at just two examples: our cities and our schools.

Just as Canada and the United States are two very different countries, so too they have very different capitals. George Washington commissioned Pierre L'Enfant to create a blueprint for a great city, one that would celebrate the republic and leave foreign visitors in awe. L'Enfant's plan, though much modified, succeeded beautifully, though it took well over a century to be realized. Built on an uninhabited swamp – as the locals still bitterly observe while swatting mosquitoes and setting out traps for rats – on the north bank of the Potomac, Washington was and is a city of neo-classical columns, great boulevards, grand vistas. It is the Capitol Dome lit at night, visible from so many parts of the city because of strictly enforced building-height restrictions. It is looking down the National Mall from the Lincoln Memorial and believing that, yes, this is the new Rome. It is the Metro, its stations ridiculously overbuilt to remind travellers that where they get on or off is not just a subway stop, it is a subway stop in the capital of the world. This is the capital America made for itself because it believed it was worth it.

Ottawa was chosen as Canada's capital because it lay on the border between Upper and Lower Canada and so represented a compromise between the English and the French. Also, it could be more easily defended from American attack than the other candidates, Montreal and Kingston. The problem with picking Ottawa – apart from the isolation, the snow, and the blackflies – was that Bytown was already there, a rough-and-ready lumber town noted for its brawls, prostitutes, and regular outbreaks of epidemic diseases. The neo-Gothic capital buildings had to accommodate themselves to what was already there. There would be no grand boulevards, no inspiring vistas. Instead, a modest capital for a modest country. Besides, although Ottawa lacked a National Mall, the rivers and the Gatineau Hills offered their own, quiet beauty, reminding the visitor that this was the capital of a country with a whole lot of wilderness and not much population. Ottawa at its best spoke of and for a people who had accommodated themselves to a tough land, while building a life and a country for themselves – no small achievement, given the obstacles. That was Ottawa's quiet pride.

In recent years, however, the two capitals have told another story, a story of renewal in one city and decline in another, a story that refutes casual and increasingly unfounded cultural assumptions, a story that should hearten Americans and alarm Canadians. Washington is flourishing as never before. Ottawa is a mess.

In 1997, the District of Columbia reached its nadir. Over the preceding decade, its population had fallen by almost 100,000, to 529,000. Middle-class blacks, as well as whites, were fleeing the city; the remaining pockets of affluence – Dupont Circle, Georgetown, Cleveland Park – felt besieged and in decline. Year after year, D.C. achieved the infamous distinction of having the highest murder rate of any metropolitan area in the nation. Large swaths of the city lay abandoned or derelict, still unrecovered from the devastating Martin Luther King race riots of 1968. Its mayor, Marion Barry, had recently spent time in prison for drug possession, after being caught on film smoking crack cocaine. His administration was so corrupt and incompetent that Congress had stripped it of most of its powers, placing the city under an appointed board of control. Washington, in other words, was the sort of city that Canadians imagined most American cities to be: a violent, hollowed-out wasteland. The only thing distinguishing D.C. from its downtrodden neighbour, Baltimore, grim setting for *The Wire*, was that it had some national museums and monuments that people visited, though nervously, and only in the daytime.

Ottawa was a different story entirely. The city was in good spirits in the late 1990s. The threat of separatism had receded and housing prices were going up. There was a new hockey arena and a new baseball stadium. The almost-new National Gallery and, across the river in Hull, the Museum of Civilization were big hits. The Byward Market was thriving, and with the new strip of bars on Elgin Street expanding, you could finally get a decent meal and party into the night without having to go over to Quebec. The city and its western satellite, Kanata, were the hub of a booming new technology sector, home to Nortel and Mitel, Cognos and Corel. The once-sleepy west end was rapidly gentrifying, as Westboro Village joined the Glebe, the Golden Triangle, and New Edinburgh as fashionable addresses. Ottawa was a classic example of enlightened policies, first put in place in the 1950s and 1960s, that had borne splendid fruit in cities across Canada. Metropolitan government ensured that the suburbs paid their fair share of the costs of keeping the inner city healthy. And immigration policies that encouraged newcomers on the one hand, but ensured that no one particular ethnicity dominated on the other, contributed to multihued, tolerant, and peaceful neighbourhoods. Canadian cities worked, and few worked better than the national capital.

But the intervening years have transformed both cities. In Washington, a confluence of forces launched an urban renaissance. The voters, finally rid of Marion Barry, elected Tony Williams, a quiet, capable expert in public policy and government finance, with a penchant for bow ties. He converted a $518 million budget deficit in 1996 into a $1.6 billion-plus surplus in 2005 and used tax abatements, bonds, and subsidies to recruit investment, some $40 billion-worth, earning Washington the title of best city in the United States for real-estate investment. He lured the Expos away from Montreal by building them a baseball stadium in a grim, rundown neighbourhood a mile south of the Capitol building, which is today a jumble of new condominiums and construction cranes. The Washington Nationals stink, but the city loves having a baseball team to complain about. Williams cleaned up the streets, got the fountains working, beefed up the ranks of the local police. Crime rates plummeted.

The new mayor's arrival coincided with and encouraged an astonishing reverse exodus. The children of the baby boomers were chafing at suburban living and the hours-long commute to and from their government jobs in the downtown. The district's housing stock remained intact: the older neighbourhoods included an attractive mix of mostly Federalist and Victorian row housing that was cheap to buy and easy to renovate. The gay community, invariably the earliest of new lifestyle adopters, flooded into Dupont Circle and began agitating for better garbage removal, improved street lighting, cleaner and safer streets. They were followed by DINKs (double-income, no kids), who settled in Logan Circle, Adams Morgan, the revitalized U-Street corridor, and Capitol Hill, reaching as far north as Columbia Heights and Shaw.

The most bewildering transformation of all occurred along Pennsylvania Avenue and the blocks north. A new hockey arena on 7th Street Northwest encouraged developers to buy up the surrounding dilapidated buildings and vacant lots and convert them to restaurants and condominiums. In the space of five years, they created an entirely new downtown district, dubbed the Penn Quarter, as vibrant now at night as it was deserted and dangerous just a few years ago.

Encouraged, the federal government and philanthropists followed with investments of their own. The new National Portrait Gallery is in the Penn Quarter.

Across the street is the International Spy Museum, while nearby, the new Harman Center for the Arts houses the superb Shakespeare Theatre Company. The Newseum, dedicated to the media, opened in 2008 beside the much-admired Canadian embassy on Pennsylvania Ave., and a beautifully restored Ford's Theatre reopened on February 12, the two-hundredth anniversary of Lincoln's birthday.

There are stresses. Lower-income black residents complain bitterly about being forced out of their homes. Now they're the ones who have to commute endlessly from the suburbs. But many other African Americans owned their homes in the city and appreciated the skyrocketing property values. And no one – *no one* – could have predicted that racial integration would finally come to Washington as a result of whites moving into black neighbourhoods. The two communities live side by side but apart, still socially segregated. But they *are* living side by side, which is something of a miracle.

Washington may be among the more impressive examples of urban renewal in the United States, but it is hardly the only one. Everyone knows the transformation Rudy Giuliani and Michael Bloomberg wrought on New York. Boston's Big Dig, however overbudget it may have been, is helping Boston bloom. Chicago is vibrant, and Denver's downtown has been reborn, making it among the most attractive cities in the United States. From Greenville, South Carolina, to Des Moines, Iowa, and beyond, inner cities are gentrifying as the young and the affluent reconnect with the pleasures of living downtown. The industrial centres of the Midwest still struggle – Detroit is a disaster, and Cleveland is troubled, though Pittsburgh is on the rebound. Even Baltimore is trying, though its lovely new (and no doubt very expensive) Inner Harbor backs onto an almost-deserted downtown that's surrounded by districts that are essentially off-limits for whites – but overall it's fair to declare that America's cities are coming back.

Ottawa, on the other hand, has had a dreary decade. As the years passed, residents slowly realized what an insane decision it had been to locate the hockey arena on the farthest edge of the city, depriving the downtown of the revitalization other cities enjoyed by situating sports facilities in troubled central neighbourhoods. In 2000, the dot-com bubble burst, leaving Nortel and other Silicon Valley North companies a shadow of their former selves, if they survived at all.

By early 2009, there were about 55,000 technology-related jobs in the region, a third fewer than at the peak of the dot-com bubble, with more cuts expected. And if that weren't bad enough, the baseball team left.

In 2005, an expanded Canadian War Museum opened in new quarters in LeBreton Flats, but a light-rail (LR) proposal fell apart over intergovernmental bickering. A new LR plan, including an east-west tunnel through the downtown, was approved in November 2008, but federal and provincial funding is now in doubt. It may never be built. Meanwhile, the city is still recovering from a two-month transit strike that lasted until February 2009. The stadium at Lansdowne Park sits mostly unused, having set what must be some kind of record for hosting failed sports franchises. Efforts to revive Rideau Street have proved a boon mainly for tattoo parlours. The new American embassy on Sussex Drive turned out to be an eyesore. Down the road, the National Capital Commission inexplicably allowed Saudi Arabia and Kuwait, neither of them close friends of Canada's, to build embassies on some the choicest real estate in the city. Worst of all, the Harper government cancelled the conversion of the former American embassy into a new national portrait gallery. There's nothing like having a government that despises its own capital.

Journalist Andrew Cohen enraged the city's boosters when his 2007 book, *The Unfinished Canadian,* described Ottawa as "a city that has given up. It bumps along, living off its past, avoiding its future. They say that New York City is a place in a hurry, a town without foreplay. Ottawa is in no hurry at all. It is a town without climax." Cohen was being too harsh, refusing to acknowledge things that were working, such as the internationally popular chamber music festival, the flush of condominium projects, the rationalization of the eleven metropolitan governments into a single city.

But he spoke to a larger truth: in central Canada, the sense of optimism has drained out of Canada's cities. Montreal still has not convincingly reversed the generation of decline that arrived with the separatists in 1976. The public spaces of downtown Toronto, which Peter Ustinov once dubbed "New York run by the Swiss," are plagued by the homeless, the appalling legacy of Ontario's decision in the 1980s to close mental institutions without providing adequate housing or community support for their former residents. Cities are dirty and getting dirtier, all the big transit projects are on hold, the expressways remain unburied while the morning and afternoon rush hours threaten to link up. There are bright spots: Toronto has a splendid new opera house and remodelled art gallery, though Daniel Libeskind's addition to the Royal Ontario Museum seems to be universally loathed. But even Toronto's most ardent boosters accept that it is a city in decline, in equal measure fought over and neglected by every level of government, blighted by homelessness and dirt, its infrastructure deficit reaching critical levels. (It would take $320 million just to eliminate the backlog in road repairs.)

Critics will find a hundred exceptions, all of them valid, but the broad truth remains. Canadian misconceptions about the failure of American cities and the success of Canadian ones are just that: misconceptions, fallacies that fail to account for the American capacity for renewal and that blind too many Canadians to the problems in their own cities. It is a price we pay for our native lack of curiosity, our unwillingness to experiment, and a federal government that long ago gave up thinking about cities, what they needed, and what Ottawa could provide.

Municipalities are, of course, dependencies of provincial, not federal, government. And past shared-cost and shared-jurisdiction programs – such as in subsidized housing, where the feds convinced the provinces and cities to participate in building projects, then decided to get out of the business, leaving the other governments with the tab – have led to wasteful spending and confusion. Yet all Canadians accept that Ottawa can and should play a role in the places in which we live, a belief that lies behind the broad acceptance of the Canadian Mortgage and Housing Corporation. Perhaps we need to reconceive the notion of infrastructure itself. Is a bridge over the Don Valley just a Toronto bridge or it is part of the national infrastructure? Is there a role for the federal government in conducting an infrastructure inventory – or, better still, asking a professional association or its equivalent to conduct it, to avoid the temptations of patronage – that would allocate federal funds directly on the basis of urgency of need rather than funnelling them through the provinces? In the U.S., the Obama administration has proposed just such an inventory, though the rushed-through stimulus package may have pushed that priority aside. There's no reason it should be pushed aside in Canada.

I am eating my own words here. In the past I have strenuously opposed federal interference in areas of provincial jurisdiction. But there's ideology, and then there are the facts on the ground. Municipalities everywhere rightly complain that they lack the revenue sources to fund themselves. But provincial governments everywhere seem unable or unwilling to provide those cities with the resources they need. In Canada, the only way for a city to get its needs met is to host the Olympics. This suggests that, under normal circumstances, provincial and federal governments are spending the money elsewhere. But are Toronto's or Winnipeg's or Montreal's or Halifax's needs any less urgent than Vancouver's? Are they penalized – deprived of funding to repair roads and sewers, upgrade public transit, sweep the streets, for heaven's sake – just because the world won't be visiting them in 2010? The obsession with Olympic upgrades suggests that governments don't focus sufficiently on the needs of their cities in normal times. Money goes elsewhere – to slake the demand from rural areas that are heavily overrepresented in legislatures, to subsidize the industries of yesterday, such as agriculture and shipbuilding, leaving cities to fend for themselves as they seek to accommodate immigrants, pay for welfare and social services, and attract and retain the jobs of tomorrow.

American cities are faced with identical problems. But, at least until the economy went into crisis, many cities had a homemade advantage: a massive increase in tax revenues from the migration back into the downtown of the next-generation middle class. The migration is much less pronounced in Canadian cities because the middle class never left in the first place.

We need to start talking about a new role for the federal government in urban affairs. There are some – though they tend to be the sorts of people who don't get out enough – who believe the provinces are anachronisms, that the proper realignment of Canadian political structures would involve a federal government interacting with a collection of regional city-states. Ain't gonna happen. But there is a visceral appeal to the idea, a recognition that our cities are the future of our country and that the provincial governments sometimes appear to be jealous of them and reluctant to encourage them. If so, then maybe Ottawa does need to become part of the urban conversation again.

Washington's downtown neighbourhoods may be unrecognizable from a decade ago, but Washington's public schools still live down to their reputation. Despite spending $13,000 per student annually, one of the highest rates in the country, the District of

Columbia Public School system routinely produces abysmal results. In a 2007 test, only 8 per cent of its eighth grade students tested "proficient" or better in math, the worst result in the United States. D.C. students also come dead last in reading scores.

Despite the influx of newcomers, Washington remains a majority-minority city: most of its residents are African American, and most of them send their children, reluctantly, to the district's public schools. Middle-class whites either send their children to private schools or to neighbourhood public schools where parents willingly supplement the school budget with their own contributions, in effect making the schools semi-private.

Although Washington's is the worst of the lot — thanks to decades of abuse of funds by board and administrative officials who treated the budget as a make-work project for themselves — inner-city school boards across the United States face the same problem: many of their students come from poor and often dysfunctional homes. Sometimes there's violence; sometimes there isn't enough to eat; more often than not there's no father. The schools themselves are often underfunded, because of the city's weak tax base, although in many cities, including

Washington, the situation is improving. And teachers unions compound the problem by insisting that teachers' pay be based purely on seniority, which means the youngest and weakest teachers are thrown into the most difficult schools. Their sole, perfectly understandable aim is to get out of the hellhole they're teaching in and make it to someplace safe, suburban, and white.

Canadian schools, compared to those in other countries, are mostly excellent. In standardized international tests administered by the Organisation for Economic Co-operation and Development (OECD), the Progress in International Reading Literacy Study and the Programme for International Student Assessment (PISA), Canadian students consistently rank among the best in the world in math, science, and reading, although we always seem to get beaten by the Finns. The latest (2007) PISA tests, for example, tested fifteen-year-old students in fifty-seven countries and subnational jurisdictions, including all OECD member states. In science, Canadian students ranked third, behind perfidious Finland and Hong Kong. The United States ranked twenty-ninth, well below the OECD average and behind such economic powerhouses as Poland, Croatia, and Latvia.

Right-wing columnists like to decry the deterioration of education standards in Canadian schools; in fact, those standards have probably never been higher. When it comes to public education, we are the envy of most of the world.

Of course, Canadians can thank their god or their lucky stars that our country wasn't afflicted with the curse of a large, racially defined underclass. Instead, we have a small one. If Aboriginals constituted 10 per cent of the Canadian population, rather than 4 per cent, and if they were concentrated in our inner cities, rather than scattered on reserves, as many Indians are, or in the North, where most Inuit live, public education in Canada might be in as sorry a state as it is in the United States.

But things are changing in American public education. Reform is in the air; new methods of teaching are producing amazing results. While Canadians congratulate themselves on their superior public schools, Americans are teaching themselves how to make the worst-performing schools into the best. The time is approaching when, once again, the Americans will have something to teach us about education.

KIPP Academy in the Bronx. Amistad in New Haven. American Indian in Oakland. Cristo Rey in

Chicago. A new kind of school is sweeping the country. Invariably, these schools are located in the toughest neighbourhoods of their respective cities. Invariably, they take in minority-race students who are under-performing. Invariably, they are able to close the achievement gap within a few years, defying all con-ventional expectations.

Take the Amistad Academy, in New Haven, Connecticut. Most of its students come from the Hill, an impoverished neighbourhood with too many drugs and too much violence. They enter the school in grade five reading at least two levels below grade level. They graduate from grade eight reading at or above grade level.

How do they do it? The same way they do it at KIPP (the Knowledge Is Power Program), which now has sixty-six schools in nineteen states, plus D.C. Eighty per cent of KIPP students are from low-income families, almost all of them black or Latino. Eighty per cent of them end up going to college.

These schools are charter schools. They are funded on a per-pupil basis by the local school board, but they are administered as non-profit, non-sectarian organi-zations. This means they don't have to hire unionized teachers or play by union rules. Once that bond is broken, anything is possible.

Now there are charter schools and charter schools. Many of them are underfunded, unfocused failures. But the charters that work – the Amistads and the KIPPs and their cousins – share a common teaching philosophy. The schools combine strict discipline with devotion to the students. David Whitman, a journalist who has written a book about this new wave in education, controversially dubbed it "the new paternalism." Students wear uniforms. The school day is longer. There are classes on Saturday morning. There is a three-week refresher course in the summer. The students are tested obsessively, to establish benchmarks and record progress. The tests also reveal which teachers get results. The best teachers get promoted; the worst are let go. Many of the teachers at these schools are products of Teach for America, a wildly successful program that takes exceptional university graduates and places them directly in schools, where their dedication and commitment more than compensate for their lack of formal training.

At Amistad, students have the teachers' cellphone numbers and are encouraged to call at night if they're having a problem with homework or if something is wrong. The principal's office is a desk in the hall. The walls are plastered with motivational slogans. The school is a refuge from the unstructured, unhappy environment the students too often confront at home. Given a choice, they prefer school. In school, they thrive.

Not all charter schools follow the same approach, and not all charter schools succeed. But the best of them, the ones that follow the KIPP and Amistad models, are rapidly eliminating the performance gap between white and minority students. They are expanding "as quickly as we can, but as slowly as we must," as one Amistad official puts it. The goals are ambitious. KIPP currently has one school in Philadelphia, but it plans to have ten by 2019. In the wake of Hurricane Katrina, New Orleans decided to go all-in with charters, as the impoverished city rebuilt its education system. More than half of all students are now educated in charter schools. The first results, released this January, revealed a 15 per cent increase in student proficiency compared to pre-Katrina results.

A wind is blowing. In Washington, Michelle Rhee, a Teach for America alumna, is trying to turn the entire public-school system into a giant KIPP. In her eighteen months on the job, she fired 270 teachers,

36 principals, and 98 administrative staff and closed almost two dozen schools in order to focus available resources on the rest. Then in February 2009, Rhee revealed the outline of a new contract for teachers. Those who wanted to could keep to the old tenured, seniority-based system. Those who opted out would be compensated based on how well they improved student outcomes. The best performers would be making $100,000 a year or more. The district's teachers union is adamantly opposed. It may not matter. A third of all Washington's students now attend charter schools.

Proposed new legislation in Florida would eliminate teacher tenure and increase pay for teachers who demonstrate skill at improving outcomes for underperforming students. School boards from Baltimore to Milwaukee to Houston have hired or are looking for superintendents who embody Michelle Rhee's philosophy or the similar approach being used by Joe Klein in New York. In California, where charter schools are proliferating, a November 2008 study revealed that twelve of the fifteen best-performing schools that cater to low-income students were charters. The Education Equality Project, an organization dedicated to the new philosophy that was chartered only this year, boasts adherents from Al Sharpton to Newt Gingrich. Obama's new education secretary, Arne Duncan, comes out of the education reform movement in Chicago.

Barack Obama himself is a believer. Not long after the inauguration, he and Michelle visited students at a D.C. charter school. And on March 10, in a major address, the president laid out the most ambitious plan to transform America's schools since the 1960s. Under Obama's proposal, teachers would be paid on merit, not seniority. Teachers who excel would receive raises; those who fail their students would be fired. The school day and school year would be lengthened. States would be encouraged to toughen their curriculums and to raise and harmonize their testing methods to create a national standard. Math and science teachers, who are in short supply, would receive higher pay than other teachers. And everywhere, state governments would encourage the expansion of charter schools.

"The time for finger-pointing is over," he told the Hispanic Chamber of Commerce. "The time for holding ourselves accountable is here. What's required is not simply new investments, but new reforms. It is time to expect more from our students. It is time to start rewarding good teachers and stop making excuses for bad ones . . . We have accepted failure for too long. Enough. America's entire education system must once more be the envy of the world."

From the classroom to the White House, there is a new approach to reforming public education in the United States. Change is coming.

I devoutly wish some civic-minded Canadian lawyer and a First Nations mother on a reserve would take the federal government to court, arguing that the appalling education her child is receiving violates his constitutional rights under the Charter of Rights and Freedoms. After all, if the Supreme Court believes, as it held in 2005 in *Chaoulli v. Québec*, that citizens have a constitutional right to adequate health care, then surely it is a constitutional abomination that, while most students in Canada receive one of the best public educations on the planet, some receive no public education at all. The federal government is responsible for education on reserves, but Ottawa has approached its responsibilities to Aboriginal education with a mixture of cowardice, incompetence, and apathy – the approach it takes to all of its other obligations to

Canada's First Nations. Money flows from Ottawa to the First Nation governments to the classroom – or not. Many reserves are too small to sustain a school based on the per-capita funding available. Sometimes, the money is diverted to other needs. Sometimes, it is wasted or worse. Many reserves have no school at all, or the building itself is condemned and the students learn in some makeshift environment, if they learn at all.

Over the past twenty-five years, despite a plethora of government studies, experiments, and programs, the on-reserve high school graduation rate hasn't improved one iota. Only 40 per cent of on-reserve Indians complete high school. Among the Inuit, the figure is 25 per cent. These figures are appalling, and the federal government, which is clearly incapable of educating Aboriginal students, should hand the money and responsibility to the provinces, which educate everyone else, and pretty well at that. And how could the provinces better educate children on reserves? Well, how about inviting in the Americans?

Alberta, that most American of provinces, is the only jurisdiction in Canada that permits charter schools. Most of its thirteen charter schools concentrate on providing extra teaching in arts or science or cater to religious minorities or gifted students, although at least one, Boyle Street Education Centre in Edmonton, focuses on at-risk youth, most of them Native. Alberta's willingness to encourage choice within its public-education system may be one reason why its students consistently outperform students in central and Atlantic Canada. But elsewhere, general contentment with the state of the system and the all-powerful teachers unions discourage reform. The unions abhor charters because teacher pay is based on merit, not seniority – though even in this respect, things are changing in the United States, as some charters unionize and unions accommodate themselves to the new reality. And, to be fair, some Ontario school boards have long experimented with alternative schools, including an all-black school that will open in Toronto in September, despite the intense controversy that surrounds the idea. Good for Toronto. Where schools are failing kids, experimentation and change must become a constant, at least until one of those changes starts producing results.

What if we went further? What if our politicians forgot about the vested interests – the unions and the school boards and the advocacy groups – and thought only about the needs of those children who are most at risk? What if they assumed, correctly, that middle-class parents always ensure that their children receive a first-class education, and focused their attention exclusively on the children who need education the most but who are least likely to get it? The Jamaican kid living in a high-rise on the edge of Toronto, with a mother who works two jobs and a father who's long gone. The kid on the fly-in reserve up north, where there are chronic problems of alcohol and drug abuse. The run-down neighbourhood dominated by Aboriginals or visible-minority Canadians who have fallen behind rather than sprung ahead. The town where the mill closed long ago and its people are still there only because their roots are too deep for them to pick up and go.

If we focused on those kids, and let the status quo take care of the rest, wouldn't we be reaching for American solutions? Wouldn't we be asking American Indian Charter schools, which have the highest test scores for any schools educating at-risk youth in California – one of them has the fifth-highest test scores of *any* school in the state – to set up a school on a reserve? Wouldn't we be looking for directors of education like Michelle Rhee, willing to take on the culture of failure?

We need premiers and education ministers who say, *Enough*. We are failing the people who need us the most. We are failing children at risk. So from now on, they are all that matter. We're going to give them good schools, with computers and science labs and musical instruments. We're going to give them the very best teachers and principals, and no one is going to earn less than six figures. We're going to bring in American non-profit organizations to run the first of these schools, until we've learned from them how it's done, and then we'll take over ourselves. And we will follow one rule: do what works, jettison the rest, and damn the cost.

If we did that, we'd see students who are testing two grades below where they should be suddenly taking off in math and reading. We'd see First Nation graduation rates soar. We'd see the children of struggling single-parent immigrant families headed for college instead of prison. We'd weaken the gangs.

To do that, though, we'd have to admit that the Americans are doing things in education that we should copy. We'd have to admit that we don't actually know what we think we know. We'd have to throw off our comfortable assumptions about why students don't learn. And we can't have that, can we?

Next thing you know, we'd be talking about increasing the role of the private sector in health care. But don't get me started.

Conclusion:

We Should Talk

ON WEDNESDAY, MAY 8, 1963, just before dawn, two firebombs smashed into Hartman Turnbow's house outside Mileston, Mississippi. While he fought the fires, his wife and daughter tried to escape, only to find armed men waiting for them outside. Turnbow grabbed his rifle and drove them off. As Taylor Branch recounts in *Parting the Waters*, the first volume of his magisterial trilogy on Martin Luther King and the civil rights movement, Turnbow had recently attempted – unsuccessfully, of course – to register to vote in Holmes County, something no Negro had tried since Reconstruction.

When Sheriff Andrew P. Smith arrived to investigate, he was confronted with an impossible dilemma for a white policeman in the South. Arresting the men who bombed Turnbow's house was unthinkable: it would mean the end of his career. Ignoring the matter was also impossible, for the FBI had arrived and were gathering evidence, and if Smith could not solve the crime himself, he would have to turn it over to them.

"These choices being unacceptable," Branch writes, "Sheriff Smith accused Turnbull of fire-bombing his own house," in order to build sympathy for the voting rights movement. For good measure, he arrested several organizers of the Negro voter-registration drive as well. The all-white jury wasted no time in finding them guilty.

On Friday, February 21, of this year, in a rural community about fifty kilometres northwest of Pittsburgh, an eleven-year-old boy allegedly shot and killed his father's pregnant girlfriend. Family members speculated he was jealous. Jordan Brown was charged as an adult, with murder and with murdering an unborn child. The shotgun he allegedly used is designed for children to use and doesn't need to be registered. After the shooting, Jordan went to school. He was in grade five.

It is as short-sighted to laud America as a shining city on a hill as it is to dismiss it as a violent imperial power in decline. Because no matter what you say about the United States, the opposite is equally true. It is a society of endless contradictions, which is the source of its dynamism. There are even more Americas than there are Canadas. Some of the Americas are actually quite Canadian. The university student sipping a latte in a Seattle coffee shop has far more in common with her counterpart in Vancouver than she does with a kid from the Shenandoah Valley attending the University of Virginia in Charlottesville. If it weren't for customs posts, it would be impossible to tell where Maine ends and New Brunswick begins. It is at the borders that Americans and Canadians seem most alike. But as you travel south, it quickly becomes apparent that theirs is a very different country, and some aspects of it are not pretty: the still-festering legacy of slavery; the passionate defence of the right to bear arms, even if those arms have nothing to do whatsoever with hunting or reasonable self-defence; a cold-hearted social conservatism that, in the name of a jealous God, persecutes gays, opposes women's reproductive rights, and retards the progress of science. The Creation Museum, which opened on May 28, 2007, in Petersburg, Kentucky, depicts a planet only 6,000 years old, where humans and dinosaurs once co-existed. The museum expected

250,000 visitors in its first year, but that many arrived in the first five months. Which shouldn't be all that surprising; only about 40 per cent of Americans believe in evolution.

Yet this is also the country whose universities are so advanced that the Europeans fear America has achieved an unbridgeable advantage in medical and other scientific research, whose foreign policy establishment is probably the most sophisticated and accomplished on earth, whose culture becomes more advanced as it becomes more dominant. The Yanks are even doing better television than the Brits now. I, for one, was inconsolable when *Battlestar Galactica* ended in March.

Sometimes it feels as though Americans and Canadians have different brains. Because their republic was forged in rebellion, defined by a civil war, shaped by a frontier mentality – because there was one for so long – American political culture is more individualistic, rougher, more open but also more competitive.

We had to do things differently. From the beginning, Great Britain had to deal with a colony the majority of whose inhabitants initially were Aboriginal and French. So a culture of accommodation developed in which everyone tried as much as possible to leave one another alone, which accounts for our lack of a sense of nationhood and for our weak central government. But complete solitude was never an option in such a harsh environment, so we came together, not in celebration of any particular national myth, but to protect our land and our families from common threats. There were so few of us, and we were so scattered, and the challenges were so great, that our biggest problems required collective solutions. While American governments gave their citizens the tools to succeed – low taxes and few regulations – Canadian governments encouraged consensus decisions and collective action, which is the only way anything gets done in this country. In the twentieth century, this approach fostered universal public health care, near-universal public education, and social programs that are markedly more generous than those south of the border. Those programs, in turn, have shaped Canadian values. The result is a society that is less affluent than the United States – for collective security punishes individual initiative – but also has fewer extremes. Two countries; two brains.

There is nothing inherently superior about America's political culture, or America in general.

Most Canadians have no desire to give up their brains and receive an American transplant. Besides, the Yanks could learn a few things from us, especially about how to run a federal election and how to make sure everyone has proper health care.

But we could learn a few things from them as well, about opening up the political process and making the public service more responsive. That has always been the case, but it has never been the case more than now, in a time when a crisis of competence infects our federal political parties and our federal public service grows ever more dysfunctional.

This book asks questions: How can we make our political parties more responsive to the public so that everyone gets to have a say in choosing a party leader and in shaping the party's policies? How can we open up the public service, making it more diverse and more attractive to people with talent and drive at all stages of their career? How can we protect both the United States and Canada from outside terrorist threats, while making it easier for goods, services, and people to cross our border freely? What can we learn from the Americans, as they set about rebuilding their once-shattered cities and their troubled public education system?

There are a couple of other things we could talk about. For one thing, should we require Members of Parliament to swear to uphold the Canadian Constitution?

Before first taking their seats, MPs must take an oath. They must swear to "be faithful and bear true allegiance to Her Majesty Queen Elizabeth the Second," the embodiment of Canadian sovereignty. In the United States, the sovereignty of the nation resides in the people themselves, which has been offered as another reason why their society is more open than ours. The president, members of the Senate, and members of the House of Representatives do not swear allegiance to the people, they swear allegiance to their constitution, the people-in-law.

Before taking her seat, a member of the House of Representatives must "solemnly swear [or affirm] that I will support and defend the Constitution of the United States against all enemies, foreign and domestic; that I will bear true faith and allegiance to the same . . ." That seems like a reasonable thing to expect. No one should sit in any parliament who is not dedicated to preserving, protecting, and defending the nation's constitution.

Quebec premier René Lévesque refused to sign the federal-provincial agreement that led to the Canada Act of 1982, which patriated our Constitution and embedded the Canadian Charter of Rights and Freedoms within it. But all Canadians are bound by the Constitution, and it is the supreme duty of every parliamentarian to protect and defend the Constitution from any threat from within or from without.

But is that what the Bloc Québécois believe? They are dedicated to the separation of Quebec from Canada. Their goal is to create a separate constitution for a sovereign Quebec. How could any member of the Bloc swear to protect the Canadian Constitution, given that the party seeks to render it void within Quebec?

The continued existence of the Bloc Québécois in the House of Commons is the single greatest impediment to the effective functioning of that Institution. They are the principal reason for a succession of unstable minority governments and contribute to the weakening of the legitimacy and authority of the federal power. Requiring MPs to swear loyalty to the Constitution might cause the Bloc to disappear in an instant. It might also create a political firestorm, giving new life to separatist forces within Quebec. Is it worth the risk, or should we just cross our fingers and hope the Bloc goes away?

Here's another question: Are there any steps we could or should take to make Ottawa matter more? Because it has surrendered so much authority in areas of domestic policy, the federal government is left with not much to do: defence, foreign affairs (although the provinces intrude here more and more), fiscal policy (though the provinces, in aggregate, may exert more influence), customs, agriculture, immigration, fisheries (horribly managed), Aboriginal affairs (a catastrophe), the environment (mismanaged in conjunction with the provinces), and criminal law. It is trying, though with indifferent success, to convince the provinces that it should regulate financial securities as well. In education, health care, welfare, municipal affairs, resource management, and transportation, it largely stands aside.

More intangibly, the various parts of Canada don't look to Ottawa anymore – if they ever did – as their government. The disparate regions increasingly self-identify, rather than considering themselves as a place within Canada. This is even becoming true of Ontario.

Anti-Americanism we all know about: it's that visceral distrust of and dislike for a country that is seen as a vulgar bully, rooted in historical difference and contemporary prejudice. It is a negative trait based on negative emotions: resentment, envy, a misplaced sense of superiority masking an ingrained feeling of inferiority. We are less likely to diagnose anti-Canadianism: an indifference toward, or dislike of, the idea of Canada. We recognize it, of course, in Quebec separatists, but the sentiment is prevalent throughout English Canada as well, and it, too, is based on negative emotions: grievance, apathy, a parochial attachment to the local over the transcendent. Newfoundlanders use it to explain decades of impoverishment; you find it around the dinner table in Calgary, as central Canada gets blamed for all ills; it explains the shoulder-shrugging dismissal by some British Columbians toward everything east of the mountains. A growing indifference to the idea of Canada may be at the very root of the steady weakening of the federal power.

At the same time, as we bring in hundreds of thousands of newcomers each year, some people fear we are losing whatever sense there is of being Canadian, of what it is we're supposed to celebrate. For this writer, the answer is clear: Canada is its Constitution, which is why all MPs and senators should swear to defend it. The Constitution embodies the values and principles that underlie its founding laws and its declaration of rights. Given how precious and hard-won those rights are, that should be good enough for any country. Others, however, believe we need to craft a more explicit and robust description of Canadian citizenship, though they have trouble explaining what, exactly, should be in that description.

Neither approach answers the question of whether Ottawa has enough to do or whether it should be doing more, whether it should seek a new national dream to inspire us or just concentrate on running the shop better. It would be nice to insert an answer here, something sweeping and noble and grand, an invocation to forge a new dominion.

Sorry, can't think of a thing to say.

But maybe you have something to say. Remember, this book is an invitation. Now that you've read it, head over to www.globeandmail.com/open&shut. You may find a message there telling you when the forum to discuss the questions arising from this book will open. You may find the discussion is already underway. I'll be contributing regularly myself, and when it wraps up, I'll write an article for the *Globe* summing up what people had to say, including what I think are the most exciting ideas.

This is an experiment. We're betting that people will engage in a substantive, productive dialogue that advances, discards, or reshapes the arguments contained in this book. We promise to do what we can to keep the crazies out. *Open & Shut* is a political pamphlet (though rather a long one). The forum will be our online coffee house. Which means this isn't really the end of this book at all. We're just moving to a different venue. And now it's your turn to talk.